W. Droth

An exciting approach to a
Study a course on God

Also use as series on Ch.life —
names of God (see revelation — ? some
men gave God because of his deal. Testimonies)
we see boldly the nature of th life of faith

Also Christology — Part II

TITLES OF

THE TRIUNE GOD

TITLES OF
THE TRIUNE GOD

Studies in Divine Self-Revelation

HERBERT F. STEVENSON

Foreword by

Paul S. Rees

FLEMING H. REVELL COMPANY

Westwood, N.J.—316 Third Avenue
London E.C. 4—29 Ludgate Hill
Glasgow C. 2—229 Bothwell Street

Foreword

STUART CHASE, one of the most articulate of American economists, has written a book he calls *The Tyranny of Words*. The new science of semantics has fascinated him. He says it has revolutionized his thinking and has altered both his writing and his speaking style. Like many another man who has been seized by a new idea, he allows himself to be carried to some absurd extremes. His voice becomes shrill—and shallow—as he shouts down the philosophers and theologians for their often opaque wordiness.

Nevertheless, Mr. Chase has gone through an experience that may well come, in some form or another, to all of us. Reading his first book on semantics—the science of *meanings* —drew from him the confession: "I looked for the first time into the awful depths of language itself."

While you are probing that sentence, make room for a reminder: God, in His self-disclosure through words (which in their Biblical expression we call the "Scriptures"), was obliged to accommodate Himself to these verbal symbols which are at once so weak and so potent. Taking the risk that lay in the frailty of words, He packed them with power. This fact, applicable to the whole range of Scripture, is singularly significant with respect to the names and titles through which He has elected to reveal Himself to men.

The Bible makes no attempt at a definition of God. What it does is to give us a wealthy *characterization* of God. This observation will grow immensely meaningful as one pursues the series which the Rev. Herbert F. Stevenson has produced for us.

When the reader has laid this volume down, he will be astonished at the number and variety of titles and metaphors through which God's character and activities are made to

5

shine. He will have a vastly enlarged appreciation of the ampleness of God, who is Creator, Redeemer, and Judge.

Mr. Stevenson has not attempted to produce a work for scholars but for students—for just plain you and me. While he has laid the work of the scholars under tribute, he has kept in mind the needs of the average reader. The result is a book which, in addition to the illumination it will immediately furnish, will send at least some of its readers off on trails of further adventure. For example, three and a half pages are devoted to the title "Jesus." Yet several chapters would not exhaust the study of this one name. The witness of the missionaries, no less than that of the scholars, could be drawn upon at length, as in the story of the aged Chinese woman who, having been released joyously from the burden of her sins through believing the "Jesus-story," came trudging back over the miles the next day, to report, ashamedly, that she had forgotten "the Name," and to implore: "Tell me, please tell me, His name again!"

How poor—how utterly, awesomely poor—the world would be without that Name!

PAUL S. REES

Introduction

NUMEROUS books have been written upon *selections* of the divine names, but I have been able to discover none dealing with all the names and titles of the Three Persons of the Trinity. Ambrose Searle, in *Horae Solitariae*, discusses the widest range of the titles that I have found in any one volume: but as he sets out to prove that all the names of God are titles of Christ, his book can hardly be regarded as an objective study of the subject! I hope, therefore, that this volume will fill a gap in Evangelical literature.

I gladly acknowledge my indebtedness to many of the extant books on the subject. Three especially provided the starting-point of the three sections of this book. *The Names of God*, by Andrew Jukes, first aroused my interest in this fascinating theme; *The Names of Jesus*, by Vincent Taylor, was—with the consent, most graciously given, of both Dr. Taylor and his publishers, Macmillan & Co.—my principal guide in the preparation of Part II; and the catena of references in Scripture to the Holy Spirit, in *Through the Eternal Spirit*, by J. Elder Cumming, provided the groundwork of Part III. In some matters of interpretation and opinion I differ from all these writers: but my debt to them is considerable. All the books included in the Bibliography have, indeed, made contribution to this: for original research is not claimed for this work. Others have laboured, and I have entered into their labours. The value of the book lies, I trust, in the fact that it gathers together what has until now been scattered through a large number of volumes, many of them difficult to obtain.

Nearly all the chapters of Part I appeared as articles in *The Life of Faith*. The difference in style of some chapters in Parts II and III, which incorporate a number of names and titles of Christ, and of the Holy Spirit, respectively, was necessary for

7

reasons of space. The classification of some of these titles was difficult, and is by no means authoritative: the selection under the various headings has been made for convenience only. These are necessarily treated briefly: fuller exposition of the contexts concerned can be found in any good commentary. It has also been impossible to supply all the Scripture references to all the titles: in most cases "key" texts only are cited—others are listed in the concordances.

To Dr. Paul Rees I would express my heartfelt thanks, not only for his Foreword, but also for the encouragement he has given me in the preparation of the book. Another of America's eminent evangelical scholars, Dr. Wilber M. Smith, Professor of English Bible at Fuller Theological Seminary, Pasadena, read the proofs during a visit to London and made most helpful suggestions. For his encouragement also I am deeply grateful. Prof. F. F. Bruce, Professor of Biblical History and Literature, University of Sheffield, kindly read the manuscript and made valuable suggestions: but that does not necessarily mean that he endorses all the views herein expressed. My thanks are due also to the Evangelical Library and its Librarian, Mr. Geoffrey Williams, who made an exhaustive search for books relevant to the subject, and placed them at my disposal. The many readers of *The Life of Faith* who urged the publication of this book will find its value enhanced, I trust, by the expansion of those chapters which they so kindly stated to be helpful when they appeared in serial form.

Contents

PART II

NAMES AND TITLES OF OUR
LORD JESUS CHRIST

PART III

NAMES AND TITLES OF THE HOLY SPIRIT

ABBREVIATIONS

ISBE—International Standard Bible Encyclopaedia
JFB Commentary—Jamieson, Fausset and Brown
IVF Commentary—The New Bible Commentary

Part I

NAMES AND TITLES OF GOD

Blessed be the name of the LORD from this time forth and for evermore—Psalm 113: 2.

"The name of God, in Scripture phraseology, is but a compendious sign for all that God has made apparent in human experience of the hidden majesty or goodness of His own nature: in a word, His 'glory.'"—J. OSWALD DYKES.

"The varying names of God are but the result of His being what He is, so wonderful and manifold that no one name can adequately express what an apostle calls His 'fullness' . . . Each differing name contains, hidden in itself (for God's perfections are inseparable), something of the special virtues which the other names bring out more separately."—ANDREW JUKES.

CHAPTER ONE

The Value of a Name

THE MANY names and titles given to God in the Bible contain a revelation of His Person and character, and His purposes toward mankind, of which even Christian people are often unaware. Names mean little to us: we use them merely as "labels" for the identification of one person from another. But in the East it is far otherwise. Bible names are significant. Some parents endeavoured to express the character of their children in the names they gave them. Plainly the parents of Nabal (which means "Fool") must have done so, in their disappointment at the earliest manifestation of his character; and years later his wife acknowledged, "As his name is, so is he; Nabal is his name, and folly is with him" (1 Sam. 25: 25). Occasionally names were changed in later life, to match the character. Our Lord was doing nothing extraordinary in giving to Simon the new name, Peter.

Of course, in the majority of cases names indicated the faith or hopes of the parents rather than the character of their offspring—*e.g.* Elijah, "*Jehovah* is God," Elimelech, "*Elohim* is King," Elisha, "Salvation is of *Elohim*," and Jehoiachin, "Strength of *Jehovah*." But the names by which God chose to make Himself known to His people are not tinged with any of our human weaknesses or limitations; they are part of the self-revelation by which, at sundry times and in divers manners, He led His people into the knowledge of Himself. "Of God as He is in Himself," writes Bishop Westcott, "in His absolute and unapproachable Majesty, we can as yet know nothing. But the names by which we are allowed to address Him gather up what is shewn to us, relatively to our powers, of His working and of His will. The divine names receive and reflect scattered

13

rays of heavenly truth as men can bear their effulgence; and when they have been set in our spiritual firmament they burn for ever. Thus each name authoritatively given to God is, so to speak, a fresh and lasting revelation of His nature. Now in one title and now in another we catch glimpses of His ineffable glory."

While there are many different names for God, each revealing some distinctive aspect of His character or grace, the phrase "the name of God" is very frequently used in the Old Testament, and stands for God Himself—the cumulative revelation of all that is made known through the various personal names. Thus, "the name of the LORD" was proclaimed to Moses on Mount Sinai, when the Lord "passed by before him" and declared Himself to be "the LORD, the LORD God, merciful and gracious, longsuffering and abundant in goodness and truth . . ." (Exod. 34: 5, 6). To "call upon the name of the LORD" was to worship Him as God (Gen. 21: 33; 26: 25, etc.); to "forget His name" was to depart from Him (Jer. 23: 27); and to "take the name of the LORD in vain" was to affront His divine majesty (Exod. 20: 7). As Dr. J. W. Thirtle said, the name of God "suggested the honour, renown, the glorious nature and holy character of the Maker of heaven and earth." Another writer says that "the name" indicates "the whole of the divine manifestation; the character of God as revealed in His relationship to His people and His dealings with them" (ISBE). This expression therefore enshrined for the people of Israel the profoundest fact of revelation and experience—that God, the Maker of heaven and earth, was specifically *their* God, who had called Israel into covenant relationship with Himself. He was the God of covenant grace. Behind every usage of the expression "the name of the Lord" lay this conviction, that He would never deny His covenant or go back on His covenant promises. His name was the pledge of all that He had promised to be to them and do for them (1 Sam. 12: 22; Psa. 25: 11).

In the New Testament, we find the name of Jesus invested with all that "the name of God" implied in the Old Testament. It contains and expresses all the values of the new covenant. Thus, sinners are saved through believing on His name (John

1: 12; 2: 23). Our Lord gave the promise that "where two or three are gathered together in My name, there am I in the midst of them" (Matt. 18: 20). He taught His disciples to pray "in My name" (John 14: 13, 14); and pledged that the Father would *give* in that name (John 15: 16; 16: 23, 24). He warned them, though, that they would be hated of all men for His name's sake (Matt. 10: 22); but promised an abundant reward for whatever of earthly relationships or possessions they might forsake for His name's sake (Matt. 19: 29).

Not surprisingly, we find in the Book of Acts the life and witness of the early Church centred in "the name." The fear-stricken leaders of the Jews penetrated to the heart of the apostolic message when they forbade Peter and John to "speak at all nor teach in the name of Jesus" (Acts 4: 18), and repeated, "Did we not straitly command you that ye should not teach in this name?" (5: 28). Beaten for this disobedience, the apostles "departed . . . rejoicing that they were counted worthy to suffer shame for His name" (5: 41); and they continued to preach "that through His name whosoever believeth in Him shall receive remission of sins" (10: 43). The rapidly growing Church was composed of "all that call on Thy name" (9: 14, 21). Paul exorcised the "spirit of divination" from the afflicted damsel at Philippi, "in the name of Jesus Christ" (16: 18); and through miracles wrought at Ephesus, "the name of the Lord Jesus was magnified" (19: 17). In his Epistle to the Romans Paul makes the glorious declaration which has been the theme of countless evangelistic sermons, from his day to this—"whosoever shall call upon the name of the Lord shall be saved" (Rom. 10: 13).

The name of the Lord—what a theme is this! It speaks to us, in this day of grace, of all that the Lord Jesus is to and for His people—Redeemer, Mediator, Head of the Church, Great High Priest, and coming King. The study of the self-revelation of God in the names by which He made Himself known, from the very beginnings of human history to the final unveiling in the Word Incarnate, should lead us to a deeper knowledge of Him, and a more adoring worship at His feet.

CHAPTER TWO

Absolute powes

Elohim—God

THERE are many names for God: for no one name could express all that He is, in Himself, and in His grace toward erring men. The study of them is not only most illuminating but, dealing with the Person of God Himself, should lead us into intimate fellowship with Him. By it, also, we enter into the heritage of all His people, in the unfolding of the progressive self-revelation of God through the ages.

First in the order of use, is *Elohim*. This is the word used in Genesis 1: 1–2: 3, and it occurs in the Old Testament some 2,550 times, which is second only to the covenant name *Jehovah*. It means, quite simply, God—as it is always rendered in the Authorized Version. The very opening words of Scripture make clear its meaning. They declare Him to be Supreme, Eternal, and Almighty; the Creator of the Universe. "It is agreed by almost all scholars," says Girdlestone, "that the name *Elohim* signifies the putter forth of power. He is the Being to whom all power belongs." And Campbell Morgan affirms that "it refers to absolute, unqualified, unlimited energy."

"In the beginning God created the heaven and the earth." The absolute monotheism of this statement, written at a time when the peoples of the world believed in many gods, bears the hall-mark of divine self-revelation, and is one of the most striking attestations of the inspiration of the Scriptures. There is not even a sidelong glance at the gods of the heathen: *Elohim* is alone the Eternal, the Almighty, the Creator; the Fount and Source of all life and being.

This matter-of-fact declaration concerning the Absolute Being and power of God is the more striking in that the word

16

Elohim is afterwards used in the Bible not only for God, but also
for the gods of the heathen. That does not mean that these are
true gods: they are merely the figments of men's minds and the
work of their hands—though behind them lurk the powers of
evil (Deut. 32: 17; 1 Cor. 10: 20). When fallen men departed
from the true self-revelation of God, they created for themselves
the gods they wanted, according to their conception of what
God is and ought to be; and in so doing they also corrupted the
divine title *Elohim*, by applying it to their gods and idols (Gen.
31: 30; Exod. 12: 12; 23: 24, etc.). God had created men for
Himself, and, estranged from Him, their hearts were restless:
but the gods they made in a vain hope of satisfying their need
were a degradation of the true revelation of God. In contrast
to them, God is ever presented in the Bible as the one true,
living God, the Creator and Lord of all.

This distinction between God and the gods of the heathen is
the theme of many a Bible story. In Egypt, Pharaoh's magicians
could simulate some of the signs which God gave of His power,
through Moses; yet in the real tests the gods of Egypt were
proved impotent, while He led forth His people by His mighty
power and stretched-out arm. Later the Philistines, having
captured the Ark of the Covenant, thought that this indicated
the greater power of their god over Israel's—until they twice
found Dagon ignominiously lying on his face before the Ark,
the second time smashed. And on Mount Carmel the issue was,
"The God that answereth by fire, let Him be God"—with the
resultant cry, "The LORD, He is the God, the LORD, He is the
God" (1 Kings 18: 39).

Elohim is a plural noun; and when God speaks, in Genesis, it
is in the plural: "Let *us* make man . . ." But the verbs used are
singular—making indisputably plain that there is no hint in
the plural noun of more than one God. This is often explained
as a "plural of majesty," just as reigning monarchs to-day, in
official proclamations and documents, refer to themselves as
"we." It is felt that "the singular number is not large enough
to set forth all that is intended, and . . . conveys an inadequate
idea of the Being whom it represents" (Girdlestone). Some

Bible students suggest that, in the use of the plural, the *manifoldness* of the Person of God is expressed. The heathen, to express his conception of God, makes many idols, for no one idol can compass all that he considers God to be. If that is so, how much more is God beyond all our thoughts of Him! All that we can conceive of God, and far, far more, is gathered up in Him—His wondrous attributes and virtues surpass our grasp of thought. This comprehensiveness of His Person, it is suggested, is conveyed in the plural noun *Elohim*.

However that may be, devout Christians have ever seen in this first of the Old Testament names of God a foreshadowing of the truth of the Holy Trinity. Not that the use of the plural noun *declares*, but rather that it *contains*, the truth that within the Godhead there is a plurality of Persons. The foundational fact established by the Old Testament is that "The LORD our God is one LORD" (Deut. 6: 4); but within the one essential Godhead there are three Persons: God is a Tri-unity. In the Old Testament, however, this was merely hinted: it could not possibly be realized or understood until the full revelation came in the Person and ministry of our Lord Jesus Christ. God is ever self-consistent, however; and even if men could not then receive it, the truth of the Trinity was indicated in the very opening words of Scripture, the very beginning of the divine self-revelation.

A simplified form of *Elohim*, *El*, is often used, and it means "The Mighty One." Examples of this are, Nehemiah 9: 32, "Now therefore, our God (*Elohim*), the great, the mighty, and the terrible God (*El*)"; and Psalm 19: 1, "The heavens declare the glory of God (*El*)." The thought that underlies both forms of the word is this—that God is almighty, able to do precisely and fully according to His will. "God said, Let there be light: and there was light. . . ." He spake, and it was done. He is the Creator and Sustainer of all.

That is the first and fundamental thing about God, which He would have us to know, and in which we find our rest. Man often boasts of his independence, and glories in his strength; but when adversity comes, his confidence fails and his strength withers. What an assurance it is at such a time, to know that God is the Rock and Refuge in whom we may hide: He is almighty, the Lord God unchanging and unchangeable, to whom we may come as did our fathers, and find in Him a very present help in time of need.

There are a few instances in the Scriptures of *Elohim* being used of men. For instance, in Exodus 4: 16 we read that God said to Moses, regarding Aaron, "Thou shalt be to him instead of God." "This phrase perfectly describes the function of a prophet, one who mediates the mind of God to the people" (IVF Commentary). Again, the word is used of judges (Exod. 21: 6; 22: 8, 9): this means that they were the representatives of God, when acting in their judicial capacity, and that those brought before them were, in effect, standing before God. In the Septuagint (the Greek version of the Old Testament) *Elohim* is translated "angels" in a few instances, notably Psalm 97: 7, and Psalm 8: 5, where man is described as made "a little lower than *Elohim*"—which the A.V., following the LXX, translates "angels," both here and in Hebrews 2: 7, where the Psalm is quoted; but the Revised Version correctly restores "God" in the Psalm.

The singular of *Elohim, Eloah,* is used principally as a poetic form of the word, and so occurs chiefly in the poetical books. It is from the same root word, we are told, as the Arabic *Allah,* and its meaning is "worthy to be worshipped." Its first use occurs in Deuteronomy 32: 15, "Then he forsook God (*Eloah*) which made him," and v. 17, "They sacrificed unto devils, not to God (*Eloah*)." That God is the one only true object of worship is a needful note, alongside that of the almightiness of God. He is not only the One to whom we can turn when in distress: He is the One whom, at all times, we should worship. He is God our Maker; we owe Him our allegiance, as the work of His hands; and we find the highest expression of our being in lifting up our hearts and voices to Him in praise and adoration.

But the only one

CHAPTER THREE

Jehovah—The LORD

SECOND only to *Elohim*, in order of appearance in the Old Testament, *Jehovah* is above every other name of God the one most precious to the Jews, and the most revealing of His grace toward His people. It is by far the most frequently used of the names of God, occurring some 6,823 times, according to the lexicographers.

A more literal translation of the Hebrew is *Yahweh*; but that is strange-sounding to us, and *Jehovah* has come to possess a distinctive value we would be reluctant to forgo. In the Authorized Version it is usually rendered LORD, in capital letters. The only exceptions are when it is joined to *Adonai* (translated "Lord"): then it is rendered GOD—Lord GOD (*Adonai Jehovah*).

The precise meaning of the name is obscure. In the Hebrew, it was originally composed of four consonants YHWH—known to theologians as "the tetragrammaton"—to which the vowels of *Adonai* were afterwards added (except when the name is joined to *Adonai*: then the vowels of *Elohim* are used). The Jews came to regard the name as too sacred to pronounce, however, and in the public reading of the Scriptures they substituted *Adonai* for it—*Jehovah* was indeed to them "the incommunicable name."

It is generally regarded as derived from the verb "to be," and some scholars suggest that it means "I am, was, and will be"—anticipating, from the very beginnings of the divine self-revelation to man, the majestic title ascribed to Him by the heavenly host: "Holy, holy, holy, Lord God Almighty, which was, and is, and is to come" (Rev. 4: 8). That is disputable, however. Dr. Campbell Morgan—in accord with the views of most Hebrew scholars—used to affirm that it is not part of the verb "to be," but of the verb, "to become," and that "its real significance is its revelation of God becoming what His people need in order to meet that need." But God's own exposition of the name makes its meaning clear—I AM THAT I AM (Exod. 3: 14). And lest there should be any doubt, He added, "Thus shalt thou say unto the children of Israel, I AM hath sent me unto you."

Whereas *Elohim* reveals Him as the Almighty, *Jehovah* sets Him forth as the eternal God—"the same yesterday, and to-day, and for ever." And more: eternal *being* is expressed in this name, I *am*. God is the ever-living One, the Fount of life. Yet another depth of meaning is contained within it, for this name also indicates the infinite glory of God, far beyond our fathoming or grasp of thought—"I am that (which) I am," as far above our comprehension as the heavens are above the earth. We shall never, in time or eternity, exhaust the revelation of His Being and grace, but we shall go on for ever discovering new glories of His Person and attributes. This name, therefore, has aptly been described as "the ineffable name."

While *Elohim* speaks of His almighty power, then, the name *Jehovah* is revealing, in part, of His character. All the moral and spiritual attributes of His Person are linked with it. No one name, of course, can fully express who and what He is: but, by manifold names, at different times and in varying circumstances, He led on His people step by step in the knowledge of Himself: the divine self-revelation was given "line upon line," as they were able to receive it.

There is a progressive revelation, indeed, in the use of this name, *Jehovah*. We first find it in Genesis 2 and 3, used *in relation to man*. Whereas He created the heavens and the earth as *Elohim*, as *Jehovah* He made man in His own image and likeness. The two names are, in fact, joined together in the story of Adam and Eve, *Jehovah Elohim* (LORD God) to make indisputably plain that *Jehovah* is *Elohim*: they are one and the same

God. (We need not, for our present purpose, take even a glance at the theory of the Higher Critics, that the two names were used by different writers, whose manuscripts were later collated.) It is significant that the only exception in Genesis 2 and 3 to the use of the two names coupled together is in the dialogue between Eve and the serpent: there *Elohim* alone— the impersonal name—is used. But when Eve bare her first son, Abel, she said, "I have gotten a man from *Jehovah*." And in Genesis 4: 26, after the sad story of the rapid degeneration of the descendants of Cain, we read concerning the godly line of Seth—"then began men to call on the name of the LORD."

Much later, when Moses had suffered his first rebuff from Pharaoh, "God said unto him, I am the LORD: and I appeared unto Abraham, unto Isaac, and unto Jacob, by the name of God Almighty, but by My name JEHOVAH was I not known to them" (Exod. 6: 2, 3). This has perplexed many people, for the name *Jehovah* occurs frequently in Genesis, as we have seen. What is meant is, that God was here investing the name with a new meaning. Before this, it had been a title—"the Self-existent One"; now it was to become a personal name. He was not merely "God," but *Jehovah*, whom they knew by name, in all the wondrous intimacy which that implies. More than that: He was entering into covenant with them, and *Jehovah* was His covenant name. It contained within itself the pledge of all that He had promised to do for them and be to them. They were to be His people, and He their God. They were to know Him in a personal, covenant relationship.

In that relationship, His self-revelation continued to be progressive—in His acts, His law, His manifold mercies. They learned that He is not only mighty to save but also able to succour; not only gracious but also holy; not only longsuffering but also uncompromising in His attitude to evil (Exod. 34: 6, 7; Num. 14: 18). They learned that, though they daily and momentarily affronted His divine majesty, yet He provided means of grace whereby they might be pardoned and restored (Psa. 106: 25, 43–45). They learned to trust Him as their

Jehovah: Being in its essence. The nature of the ultimate is connoted in this word. Not so much his character as what he IS — what accepts the IS key.

JEHOVAH—THE LORD

23

Shield and Defender in time of distress; and to fear Him as one
who chastized them for wrongdoing.

In those years of gradual unfolding of His will and purposes
and grace, the name *Jehovah* took on ever new meanings for
them: and to express these, other names were attached to
Jehovah—such as *Jehovah-rapha*, "the LORD that healeth";
Jehovah-tsidkenu, "the LORD our righteousness"; *Jehovah-nissi*,
"the LORD my banner," etc. We shall consider some of these
later on.

Upon the foundations of this knowledge of the LORD gained
in the wilderness, Israel in the land of promise proved Him to
be all that His name *Jehovah* had pledged—One who, almighty
and unchanging, was indeed "the glory in the midst and a wall
of fire round about"—so long as His people were true to the
covenant into which they had entered with Him: but One who
also was jealous of His rightful place as the Lord their God, and
would by no means ignore their sin. And as the people apprehended what He was to them, they began to express their faith
in the names they gave their sons—Jehoram, "exaltation of
God"; Jehoshaphat, "God judges," etc.

A contraction of *Jehovah*, JAH, is used some fifty times in the
Hebrew Scriptures, and is always translated LORD in the
Authorized Version with the single exception of Psalm 68: 4,
where it is transliterated. It seems to express the thought of
gladness on the part of His people, in the realization of what
God is and does for them. It first occurs in the Song of Moses—
"*Jah* is my strength and song, and He is become my salvation"
(Exod. 15: 2; cf. Isa. 12: 2; 26: 4, *Jah Jehovah*). And "Praise
ye the LORD," occurring some twenty-five times in the Psalms,
is "Hallelu-*jah*."

And finally, God who had revealed Himself "at sundry times
and in divers manners," came in the Person of His Son to make
Himself fully known—Jesus, whose name is an abbreviation of
Jehoshua, "Jehovah the Saviour." In Him, we behold the Lord
our God. He declared Himself to be the "I am"—again and
again assuming that divine title, with all that it implied
(John 8: 58). He is the living One, having life in Himself

(John 5: 26), who, in the inexpressible wonder of His grace, became dead, for us men and our salvation, but who is alive for evermore (Rev. 1: 18). In Him, we know and adore the One who made us, from whom and in whom we live and move and have our being: Jesus, the same yesterday, and to-day, and for ever; the eternal, unchangeable Lord; our Redeemer and our King.

CHAPTER FOUR

Adonai—Lord

ANOTHER name of God which, like *Elohim*, is mostly used in the Bible in its plural form, is *Adonai*, though the singular, *Adon*, is also found. It is translated in the Authorized Version "Lord"—in small letters, distinguishing it from LORD (*Jehovah*). Occurring some 340 times, it has a special interest in that, to the Jews, this was the most familiar of the names for God, since—as we have already seen—they always substituted it for *Jehovah*, which they regarded as too holy to pronounce.

The plural form, *Adonai*, is used only of God; but the singular, *Adon*, is used also of men: and its true meaning is indicated by its application to men. It is used only in connection with two classes of men: the master of slaves, and the husband of a wife. It is expressive, therefore, of a *personal relationship*—a relationship of authority, on the one hand, and of allegiance and love on the other.

These two associations of the word are deeply significant. The slave was, in Old Testament times, the absolute possession of his lord. He had no personal rights: his entire concern was to fulfil the will of his master. But that was only one side of the coin: his master also had responsibilities toward him. His wants were his master's care. We must not think of the slaves in ancient Israel in terms of "Uncle Tom's Cabin." Some were badly treated, undoubtedly; but on the whole slaves were regarded as members of the household. They had privileges denied to hired servants. Their relationship to their master was not only one of allegiance, but frequently also of love.

Even more clearly is the relationship between God and His people symbolized by that between husband and wife (Psa. 45). Sarah called Abraham "lord" (Gen. 18: 12), but not in any

25

craven subservience! Yet the word was a true expression of devoted submission, and no mere lip-service. So does God the Lord claim the obedience and loyalty of those who truly love Him (Isa. 54: 5). This, of course, is contrary to the spirit of our present age, which is characterized by independence and self-will. Few are ready to pray, sincerely, concerning all the interests and aspects of life, "Thy will, not mine, be done."

The first occurrence of the name *Adonai* in the Bible is in Genesis 15: 2 and 8, in the story of God's covenant with Abram following the deliverance of Lot, and God's renewal of His promise to give Abram a seed. Although his faith was sorely tried by the long delay in the fulfilment of the promise, Abram bowed in heart and mind before the *Lord*, in unquestioning devotion. He rested upon the divine pledge, and the sufficiency of the divine power and grace.

Equally illuminating is the use of this name for God by Joshua, when Israel was humbled by defeat through sin and pride, at Ai (Joshua 7: 7). On entering Canaan, Joshua knew that they could not conquer the land by themselves: he went forward in faith in God's promises. And the conquest of Jericho abundantly justified that faith. Then came the shattering blow of defeat by the comparatively few inhabitants of the insignificant little town of Ai. It could only mean that God was not only *not* with Israel, but *against* them. In a consciousness of utter weakness and dependence, Joshua cast himself on his face before the Lord. In Him lay Israel's one hope: at His feet, Joshua made acknowledgement that the issues of battle were in His hands. And as the *Lord*, He gave orders for the purging of the camp of Israel, and for the battle against their enemies.

Gideon, when called from obscurity to deliver Israel from oppression, signified his consciousness of utter dependence upon God by the use of this name; and from the *Lord* he received his commission (Judges 6: 13, 15). David, in various crises of his career, made confession of his sins unto *Adonai*, and looked to Him for needed deliverance and strength and help (2 Sam. 7: 18; Psa. 35: 23; 38: 9; 40: 17; 51: 15, etc.).

A particularly interesting instance of the use of the name is

Amen !

nam word of Divine Sovereignty *The True King .. the* *enpus* *wored in her absolute law, authority*

ADONAI—LORD

in Isaiah 6, where the prophet, in the year that King Uzziah died, "saw the Lord *(Adonai)* sitting upon a throne, high and lifted up" (v. 1), and at that vision cried out in awe, "Woe is me! for I am undone . . . for mine eyes have seen the King, the LORD of Hosts *(Jehovah-sabaoth)*." But note that he goes on to add, "Also I heard the voice of the Lord *(Adonai)* saying, Whom shall I send . . .?" The vision and the voice of the divine majesty and authority was the vision and the voice of the Lord *(Adonai)*. He occupies the eternal throne, and exercises an abiding sovereignty, unaffected by the vicissitudes of human life.

He made the Cov. with Abrah. ?. its secure, dependable ? irrevocable by any other authority.

Many other passages could be cited from the Old Testament, to illustrate further this significance of the name; but we must conclude with a reminder that this title "Lord" is the one ascribed most frequently in the New Testament to our Saviour, the Lord Jesus Christ—for the Greek word *Kurios* is the counterpart of the Hebrew *Adonai*. In one of His most arresting conversations with His disciples, He said, "Ye call me Master and Lord, and ye say well; for *so I am*." And such He is to all who claim Him as Saviour.

Curios

In confession before God, on behalf of His children of old, the prophet acknowledged sadly: "O Lord our God, other lords beside Thee have had dominion over us . . ." but he went on to give the pledge: "but by Thee only will we make mention of Thy Name" (Isa. 26: 13). He only has the right to our supreme love and loyalty: for He is the King of kings and Lord of lords. It is our highest privilege, as well as our plainest duty, to acknowledge Him to be "My Lord and my God."

CHAPTER FIVE

Some Descriptive Titles—Rock, Fortress, etc.

SEVERAL names for God of a descriptive or metaphorical character occur in the Old Testament, which may be grouped together. Foremost among these word-picture titles are a few which display the power and might of God, especially in the *protection* of His chosen people.

(i) ROCK (*Tsur*). Five times in the Song of Moses (Deut. 32: 4, 15, 18, 30, 31) this term is used, denoting the "eternal strength and unchangeableness" of God (IVF Commentary); it is a favourite expression also of David and Isaiah (Psa. 18: 31, 46; 28: 1; 62: 2, 7; 78: 35; 89: 26; 92: 15; 95: 1. Isa. 17: 10; 30: 29—where it is translated in A.V., "mighty one"; 44: 8—translated "God"; 51: 1). It is the ordinary word for "rock"—*i.e.*, it is used concerning the rock on which Moses stood when granted a vision of God (Exod. 33: 21, 22); and the rock in Horeb from which water flowed, when Moses smote it —"which rock was Christ" (Exod. 17: 6; 1 Cor. 10: 4). *Tsur* is also translated "strength" in the A.V. of Psa. 19: 14, "O LORD, my strength and my redeemer" (R.V. has "rock"). The granite strength of rocks, so unassailable and enduring, impressed men from the beginning of human history, and so became a fit symbol of the illimitable strength and immutable stability which are to be found in God alone. To a people on the march, amid all the hazards of a journey through the wilderness, it was inexpressibly reassuring to realize that the God in whom they trusted was the almighty and unchangeable Lord of heaven and earth. And at all times, whenever conscious of their own weakness, they would remind themselves of His steadfastness and strength. Thus David, amid the perils of war, delighted to lift his eyes from the uncertainty and unreliability of people and circumstances around him, to the rock of his salvation. He also used another word, likewise translated "rock," *sela*, which means literally "cliff"—cf. Psa. 18: 2; 40: 2; 42: 9. Matthew Henry says, "God is the rock, for He is Himself immutable and immoveable; He is to all that seek Him and fly to Him an impenetrable shelter, and to all that trust in Him an everlasting foundation."

For the perfect comment upon this aspect of the divine grace, however, we must go to the book of Isaiah—"Thou hast been a strength to the poor, a strength to the needy in his distress, a refuge from the storm, a shadow from the heat. . . . Trust ye in the LORD for ever: for in the LORD JEHOVAH (*Jah Jehovah*) is everlasting strength" (Isa. 25: 4; 26: 4). "Everlasting strength" should be translated, as in the margin, "the rock of ages"— words to which Toplady has given a somewhat different connotation, in his hymn, "Rock of ages, cleft for me"—an allusion, of course, to the "clift of the rock" in which Moses sheltered, when the glory of the LORD passed by (Exod. 33: 22). Isaiah, however, in these verses extols the manifold grace of God expressed in this figure of speech—the strength, succour, refuge from the storm and shelter from the noon-tide heat, which He affords His people. The prophet repeats the thought of the rock providing shadow in his great Messianic passage beginning "A king shall reign in righteousness," for he goes on to say, "and a man shall be as an hiding place from the wind, and a covert from the tempest . . . as the shadow of a great rock in a weary land" (Isa. 32: 2). We in the West little realize what such shadow from the blazing heat of the Eastern midday sun can mean to a weary traveller. In this verse, Isaiah declares that what God had been to His people in their every time of need, He would be in yet greater fullness of grace in the Messiah, His Anointed: and all this, indeed, Christ is to us (see p. 158).

(ii) FORTRESS (*Metsudah*). Closely allied to "rock"—and generally used in conjunction with it—is the term "fortress" as a descriptive title of God: "The LORD is my rock, and my fortress" (2 Sam. 22: 2; cf. Psa. 18: 2; 31: 3; 91: 2. Also 144: 2). This is a military metaphor, describing a mountain fastness in time of war: so it is not surprising that it makes its first appearance in Scripture on the lips of the warrior-king. David owed his life to the "place of safe hiding," the cave Adullam (1 Sam. 22: 1). Jeremiah uses another word, *maoz*, also meaning "stronghold," and translated "fortress" in our versions—"O Lord, my strength and my fortress" (Jer. 16: 19). In the conflicts of life, God has ever proved Himself to be a refuge and hiding-place of His people. Precisely the same thought is contained in Proverbs 18: 10, "The name of the Lord is a strong tower: the righteous runneth into it, and is safe." Martin Luther captures the spirit of this metaphor in his famous hymn:

> A mighty fortress is our God,
> A bulwark never failing;
> Our Helper He, amid the flood
> Of mortal ills prevailing . . .

(iii) SHIELD (*Magen*); BUCKLER (*Tsinnah*); and SWORD (*Chereb*). Long before the turbulent times of David, the term "shield" had been used concerning God—by God Himself: "Fear not, Abram: I am thy shield . . ." (Gen. 15: 1). And Moses, addressing the assembled company of the children of Israel, also used this figure of speech—and added another to it: "O people saved by the Lord, the shield of thy help, and the sword of thy excellency!" (Deut. 33: 29). David, naturally, delighted in this thought of God as the defence of His people, and on occasion linked together the two words "shield" and "buckler"—the latter being a larger type of shield (Psa. 3: 3; 28: 7; 33: 20; 35: 2; 59: 11; 84: 9; 115: 9; 119: 114; 144: 2). Here is a double protection, indeed, from the "slings and arrows" of the enemy! The Apostle Paul gives a somewhat different application to the thought of God's protecting care, in his references to the Christian's panoply, including the "shield of faith" (Eph. 6: 11–17); but the underlying truth is the same, that the Lord is the defence of His people, in the adversities of life, and from the assaults of Satan.

(iv) MIGHTY ONE (*Abhir*, and *Gibbor*). Two Hebrew words are translated "mighty one" or "strong one" in our English versions; but the first of these—*abhir*—is, most interestingly, used only in conjunction with the names "Jacob" and "Israel" —"the mighty one of Jacob" (Gen. 49: 24; Psa. 132: 2, 5; Isa. 49: 26; 60: 16); and "the mighty one of Israel" (Isa. 1: 24). This phrase was first used by Jacob (Israel) himself, on his death-bed, in the blessing of his beloved son Joseph—"But his bow abode in strength, and his hands were made strong by the hands of the mighty God of Jacob." It is a remarkable testimony to God; and an equally remarkable expression of simple, unfeigned faith in the God who had been with him all the days of his life, unworthy though he knew himself to be— for was he not Jacob, "the supplanter"? As thus used by the dying patriarch, "the mighty God of Jacob" might well be paraphrased, "The God whom I have experienced to be mighty, alike in His forbearance and His faithfulness, in all the varied experiences of my life; who has also been with my son, as He has been with me; the God who will continue to be mighty, I am confident, in His blessings toward Joseph, in all the future days." Grace received ever begets confidence in grace to come!

It is suggestive that this expressive phrase, "mighty God of Jacob," should be used by David in His prayer concerning the sanctuary which he aspired to build for the Lord in Jerusalem (Psa. 132: 2, 5), probably realizing that many who would gather in the temple-to-be would have much of "Jacob" in them! And Isaiah used the term in pronouncing the divine judgment upon the oppressors of God's people: seemingly so insignificant, and so easy a prey for their powerful neighbours, they were yet the special concern of "the mighty God of Jacob."

The second word translated "mighty one," *Gibbor*, is used by David in expressing assurance that God would fight for Israel against their enemies (Psa. 24: 8; 45: 3). This adjective is frequently applied to "mighty" men, and implies exceptional physical strength and prowess. Its first application to God was made by Moses, when he sought to impart to the generation of Israelites which had been born in the wilderness, and therefore had not experienced the wonders of the Exodus nor witnessed the terrors of Sinai, a sense of the majesty and unique glory and power of God—"For the LORD your God is a God of gods, and Lord of lords, a great God, a mighty and terrible . . ." (Deut. 10: 17). Isaiah and Jeremiah also use the term (Isa. 10: 21; 42: 13; Jer. 32: 18). The irresistible power of God, not so much in His eternal omnipotence—which is expressed in the title *Elohim*—but *on behalf of His people*, is graciously conveyed in both of these dynamic titles, *Abhir* and *Gibbor*. The most significant use of *Gibbor*, however, is in Isaiah's prophecy concerning the Messiah, "the Mighty God," *El Gibbor* (Isa. 9: 6; see p. 107).

(v) STRENGTH (*Netsach*). A most interesting title is ascribed to God by Samuel—"The Strength of Israel" (1 Sam. 15: 29). The exact meaning of *netsach* is somewhat difficult to define; in the A.V. it is translated by no fewer than three nouns—blood, strength, and victory; and five adjectives—always, constantly, ever, evermore, and perpetual. The root meaning, as far back as can be traced, appears to bear the twofold sense of *eminence* and *duration*. Twice it is used concerning human strength (Isa. 63: 6; Lam. 3: 18); but only in 1 Samuel 15: 29 is it a title of God. Commentators differ widely in their views of its significance in this phrase. S. R. Driver suggests "The Glory of Israel"; JFB, "He that gives a victory to Israel"; and Ellicott's "The Changeless One of Israel"—a rendering in keeping with the thought of *duration*, expressed in the adjectives "constantly" and "perpetual." The context is the story of Saul's disobedience to the divine command in sparing Agag, and the consequent rebuke by Samuel, and intimation that "the LORD hath rent the kingdom of Israel from thee . . ." Samuel proceeded to emphasize the irrevocability of this judgment, for "the Strength (or, Changeless One) of Israel will not lie nor repent . . ." Now, in v. 11 we are told that the LORD had said to Samuel, "It repenteth me that I have set up Saul to be king . . ." This is one of the many instances in the Bible of God's acts being explained anthropomorphically— that is, in terms of our human experiences and emotions, so that we might understand. But the truth is, as Samuel stressed, that "God is not a man, that He should repent"—*i.e.*, change His mind. He is the Eternal, the Changeless One; He knows the end from the beginning: but in the outworking of His eternal purpose He sometimes *appears*, according to our human judgment, to repent, or change His mind. It is not He who has changed, however, but men. He does not deal with any as with automatons, but according to their response to His purposes and grace. Saul had his opportunity, and failed; but he was not denied his opportunity because God foreknew that he would fail. Because of that failure, however, God "repented" that He had set up Saul to be king. He withdrew the high privilege He had conferred upon Saul, but did not "lie nor repent" in doing so. Something of the sorrow of God in the defections of His children is conveyed by the word; a sorrow none the less real because the defections are foreseen and foreknown.

This is another of the several titles which express the severity and goodness of God as complementary aspects of His character. How comforting it is to know that the Eternal is the Changeless One! But to the wayward, like Saul, it is an awesome realization that He knows beforehand the outcome of all our decisions and doings, and has determined our destiny accordingly. Yet in His severity there is goodness, for all—like Saul— have their opportunity: none is "predestined" by God to rejection. But He is never taken by surprise; never caused to "repent" as men do. His tender grace is revealed in that He *seems* to repent: He truly sorrows in our failings and failures. But even divine grace has its limits: there is a sin involving irreparable loss. When judgment is pronounced upon it, there is no escape: it is a judgment in accord with His character as the Changeless One; there can be no "repenting" of it on His part. For God is not a man, that He should be persuaded or coaxed; nor are His judgments affected by varying moods, for He is the *Changeless* One. Stern as that word may seem to the guilty, it is nevertheless the foundation of eternal security; for if His judgments were subject to a whim, or to any of the considerations which sway our human reactions to facts and situations, then we could never be *sure* of our standing and estate before God. But as James declared, long afterwards, with Him is "no variableness, neither shadow of turning." Despite its context of judgment, therefore, this title has as its deepest note the comfort and assurance of those who "trust and obey." Three further descriptive titles, of quite a different character, are:

(vi) JEALOUS (*Kanna*). In the first of the ten commandments the LORD declared Himself to be "a jealous God" (Exod. 20: 5); and in Exod. 34: 14 this strong term is elevated, from an adjective, into a name of God—"for the LORD, whose name is Jealous, is a jealous God." These, and the three other occasions on which this word is used (Deut. 4: 24; 5: 9; 6: 15) are all in connection with the divine command that Israel should worship God alone, and not the gods of the heathen. While this is so, however, the original conveys none of the rather sinister meaning which "jealous" has come to possess. The word has changed its meaning somewhat since it was selected by the translators of the Authorized Version for use in these passages; it then meant —as the original does—*zealous, rather than "jealous."* "This word did not bear the evil meaning now associated with it in our usage, but rather signified 'righteous zeal,' Jehovah's zeal for His own name or glory (cf. Isa. 9: 7, the zeal of Jehovah; also Zech 1: 14; 8: 2)" (ISBE). And the IVF Commentary observes—"*A jealous God.* Not in the sense that He begrudges success or happiness to others, but He alone has a claim upon the love of His people. It is for their sakes, that they may hallow and reverence His name, that they must flee idolatry. God's jealousy preserves the purity of His people's worship."

(vii) EL-ELOHE-ISRAEL. One of the most moving of the names for God was given by Jacob to the altar which he erected in Shechem, at his first encampment in the promised land after his return from long exile in Padan-aram—*El-Elohe-Israel,* "God is the God of Israel" (Gen. 33: 20). This was both a courageous testimony and a heart-stirring affirmation of faith. Jacob had returned to the land from which his own duplicity had driven him, long years before. His heart had been full of fear at the prospect of meeting his brother Esau and the consequences of his former sins. But during his journey the LORD had met him, and after an all-night struggle Jacob had greeted the dawn limping, but with a new name—Israel, Prince with God. On the strength of that experience, and in reliance upon the work of grace wrought in his life, he went forward. At the first opportunity he erected an altar, declaring both his faith and his transformation of character. He worshipped, acknowledging God to be *his* God; and himself to be a man of God—indeed, a prince with God. Following in his train, myriads of "Jacobs" have trusted and worshipped and witnessed, that God—the living Lord of heaven and earth—is their God; and that He has wrought in them the miracle that makes a Jacob into an Israel.

(viii) EL-BETHEL.   The reality of the transformation of Jacob into Israel was further attested by his return, at the command of God, to Bethel—where he had first met with God, in the vision of the ladder from heaven to earth. On that occasion he had realized as never before that God is indeed the living God; and that the very wilderness is "the house of God" to those aware of His presence (Gen. 28: 11–22). There Jacob had, for the first time in his life, truly worshipped, and made his vows unto God. Now he had returned, and by the name he gave to the altar he erected—*El-Bethel*, "The God of the house of God," Gen. 35: 7—he re-affirmed his faith in the God who had met him years before. Therein lie two lessons of abiding worth. First, that despite all the deviations of our walk through life, we may ever return to the God who met with us years ago, for He is unchanging and unchangeable. And we may ever come to Him knowing that He will be to-day what we have proved Him to be in time past. Whatever we have experienced of His grace, in His sanctuary, He is ready to be to us in our present condition and need. Some people look wistfully back to a spiritual experience in the long ago: an occasion when the house of God became indeed the gate of heaven. But they have wandered far since then; they have neglected their vows and forgotten the vision of an opened heaven. Now it seems impossible to return. Jacob testifies across the centuries, however, that so long as life shall last it *is* possible to return: for God is ever, unchangeably, the God of Bethel—as ready to meet with us in grace to-day as He did when first He spoke to us, and opened our eyes to that which is unseen and eternal. For He is *El-Bethel*.

CHAPTER SIX

El Shaddai—God Almighty

God-being-power + his disposition deed

MOST OF the Old Testament names of God are made up of two words—*El* (the shortened form of *Elohim*) or *Jehovah*, and another word added, revealing some specific attribute or grace of God, or facet of His character. In these composite titles, the first part has the full wealth of meaning which we have seen *Elohim* and *Jehovah* to possess: but with some further unfolding of His Person, or will, or provision for His people.

One of the most tender of these composite names is *El Shaddai*, rendered in the Authorized Version as "God Almighty." That is, however, a most inadequate translation which quite misses the profound implications of this wondrous title, and the revelation of the love of God toward His creatures which it contains. It is true that the Almightiness of God is expressed in the first part of the name—for *Elohim* means "the Mighty One," as we have seen. To that, however, is added the further thought expressed in the second word. What, then, is the significance of *Shaddai*?

It is so old a word that its original meaning is obscure. Some Hebrew scholars assert that it means "strong," or "mighty"— or "signifying the God who is manifested by the terribleness of His mighty acts," as the International Standard Bible Encyclopædia suggests. Some such view was evidently adopted by the translators of the Authorized Version, when they rendered it "God Almighty." Other speculations favoured by scholars are succinctly stated by H. L. Ellison—"The two most likely etymologies would both bring out the power of God, and so justify the Greek rendering. The simplest would link it with *shadad*, to devastate, and so lay stress on the irresistible power of

God. The most popular to-day, one going back to Hommel and strongly supported by Albright, would link it with a word not found in Hebrew, but extant in Akkadian, *shadu*, mountain, *i.e.*, He of the Mountains." We consider all these suggestions profoundly unsatisfying. As to the latter, we cannot accept the implication that God was regarded as "the God of the mountains." There is nothing whatsoever in the contexts, in the majority of cases, to warrant such a conception. As to the former, "the Devastator," this, like the "God Almighty" of the A.V., would add practically nothing to *Elohim*, which declares Him to be the mighty God. Why we should adopt a speculation which would "justify the Greek rendering" passes our comprehension!

What we accept to be the true meaning gives to this title a value distinctive from all others in the Bible—and one so arresting and fitting that it is surprising to find these pundits reluctant to acknowledge its validity. For we adhere to the traditional view that *Shaddai* is derived from the word "invariably used in Scripture for a woman's breast" (Scofield). The singular form, *shad*, is translated in the Authorized Version by three words—"breast" (eighteen times), "pap," and "teat." As applied to God, it therefore becomes a graphic metaphor: He is "the Breasted One." This has emboldened some Bible students and preachers to speak of "the Mother-love of God."

Dr. Campbell Morgan says, "The name or title *El Shaddai* is peculiarly suggestive, meaning quite literally, 'the mighty One of Resource or Sufficiency.' We miss much of the beauty by our rendering, 'God Almighty.' The idea of almightiness is present, but it is fully expressed in the word *El*. The word *Shaddai* goes further, and suggests perfect supply and perfect comfort. We should reach the idea better by rendering 'God All-bountiful,' or 'God All-sufficient.' ... To gather sustenance and consolation from the bosom of God is to be made strong for all the pilgrimage. ..."

Canon Girdlestone writes in almost identical terms—"The title *Shaddai* really indicates the fullness and riches of God's grace, and would remind the Hebrew reader that from God

cometh every good and perfect gift—that He is never weary of
pouring forth His mercies upon His people, and that He is
more ready to give than they are to receive. The word is connected with a root which signifies a breast, and hence the idea
is similar to that contained in our word exuberance. Perhaps
the expressive word 'bountiful' would convey the sense more
exactly."

El Shaddai, then, is a most tender title, used of God exclusively
in relation to His children. To the baby, the mother is the all-
sufficient one. At her breast he nestles, warm and secure, and
there he finds his sustenance. In a word, there his every need
is met. By the vivid imagery of this title of God, His providential grace is most graphically portrayed. He is the Succourer
and Satisfier of His people.

The first use of the term in Scripture—as is almost invariably
the case with all the different names of God—brings out clearly
its distinctive significance. It occurs in Genesis 17: 1, where
Abram, after long testing, had come to an end of his self-
sufficiency, and all hope of realizing the promise and purpose
of God (that he should have a son) in his own strength. In that
hour of long-deferred hope and unfulfilled expectation, "the
LORD appeared to Abram and said unto him, I am the Almighty
God: walk before Me, and be thou perfect. And I will make
My covenant between Me and thee, and will multiply thee
exceedingly." There is no hint here of either "The God of
devastation" or "The God of the mountains"! Rather, He is
the One, mighty and gracious, through whose love and power
alone the promise would be fulfilled. *El Shaddai!* As the name
fell upon human ears for the first time, it must have sounded
like music indeed, giving Abram an altogether new understanding of God—of His heart of love; His compassionate
understanding; His abundant power to fulfil the impossible;
His delight in imparting the best of gifts to His child.

Abraham must have passed on to his son something of what
he learned of God in this crisis of his career; for when Isaac
came to the time of separation in his family, with all that
it meant in the sending away of Jacob to find a bride, he

dismissed him with the words, "God Almighty bless thee . . ." (Gen. 28: 3). The break-up of a family; the going away of a son, perhaps never again to be seen in this life, is always a most profoundly moving experience. What comfort at such a time can compare with that of knowing that the departing one is under the care of the Almighty, *El Shaddai.*

And Jacob, in his turn, found in this same name his greatest consolation when blessing *his* son, Joseph (Gen. 49: 25, 26).

A deeply moving use of the name is found in the Book of Ruth. When Naomi returned to Bethlehem after long years and sorrowful experience in Moab, she was greeted with surprise by those who remembered her. "Is this Naomi?" To which she replied, in bitterness of spirit, "Call me not Naomi (which means 'pleasant'), but call me Mara ('bitterness'), seeing the LORD hath testified against me and the Almighty (*Shaddai*) hath . . . afflicted me" (Ruth 1: 20, 21). If the God of tender grace had dealt bitterly with her, what hope or expectation had she? But the very name she used to express her despair contained within it, had she ears to hear, the note of hope: He is indeed *El Shaddai,* and proved Himself so to her!

Out of the forty-eight occurrences of the name in the Old Testament, thirty-one are found in the Book of Job. That fact is arresting. It is not just that the writer of "Job" was fond of this name of God: the Holy Spirit, the Author of the entire Scripture, designed it so. For no Old Testament book more wonderfully reveals the mighty, tender love of God for His child, than "Job" does.

The keenest part of the travail of Job was the thought—so bluntly and cruelly stated by his "friends"—that the *Almighty* had stricken him. If *such* a God were chastening him so sorely, they inferred, he must be wicked indeed! The anguish of Job lay in the fact that he knew his own integrity, and could not understand why the God whom he loved and trusted should deal with him so. He had sought sincerely to worship and serve *El Shaddai*—yet this calamity had happened to him. But because he truly knew Him to be *El Shaddai,* and despite the taunts of

his accusers, he held on to the truth concerning the character of
God as he had come to know Him, and was able to rise above
his anguish to the sublime height of faith, in the declaration,
"Though He slay me, yet will I trust in Him."

The child of God who knows Him as *El Shaddai* will always
be able to do that. In times of testing He may seem to be far
otherwise than the "Father of mercies and God of love"; but
faith rests upon the assurance and the verity that God is indeed
good, and that in the end we shall say with thanksgiving, "He
hath done all things well." For what His goodness plans, His
power perfects. He is God Almighty, *El Shaddai*.

CHAPTER SEVEN

El Elyon—The Most High God

EVERY name for God has a distinctive meaning and value,
however similar it may seem to be to another title, in our
English rendering. Thus *El Elyon*—translated in the
Authorized Version as "the Most High God"—appears to be
practically synonymous with *El Shaddai*, "the Almighty"; but
that is not the case. Both are titles of the same God, of course;
but they reveal different aspects, or facets, of His character
and grace. We have seen that the translation of *El Shaddai* is
misleading; but *El Elyon* is rightly translated "the Most High
God," for it speaks of Him as "high over all," supreme and
omnipotent.

In Psalm 91: 1, *El Elyon* is linked with *El Shaddai*—"He that
dwelleth in the secret place of the Most High shall abide under
the shadow of the Almighty." That is a wonderfully reassuring
juxtaposition of these two divine titles. The thought of the
absolute authority and power of God, expressed in the name
El Elyon, might cause us to fear and tremble before Him: but
the Most High is also *El Shaddai*, the Fount of all grace and
mercy. More than that: *El Elyon* is able to do all He wishes
and wills as *El Shaddai*. Our good intentions are all too often
frustrated by our limitation of power or skill: but no one and
no thing can withstand or thwart the purpose of the Most
High.

This name is first introduced to us in the Bible by Melchizedek
(Gen. 14: 19). After Abram's conquest of the five kings,
Melchizedek blessed him in the name of the Most High God,
"possessor of heaven and earth." That phrase throws a flood
of light upon the name. It shows that He is not—as the Deists
taught—so high and aloof as to be unconcerned with people

42

and events on this tiny part of His vast universe. He is indeed high and holy: the Most High; but He is also the sovereign Lord, who rules in all the affairs of men. The victory of Abram over Chedorlaomer and his allies had been given by God. He is, through all the vagaries and vicissitudes of human life, working His purposes out.

Isaiah gives us a glimpse into another realm, however; and into events long before the creation of this world, when he tells us of the sin of Lucifer, son of the morning, who, lifted up in pride, said in his heart, "I will exalt my throne above the stars of God . . . I will ascend above the heights of the clouds; I will be like the Most High" (Isa. 14: 12–14). The word "ascend," in this text, is literally "go on high." Lucifer aspired to usurp the eternal throne; to occupy the place of the Most High. But no matter how he might aspire, he could never *be* the Most High: there is One, and only One, who is, eternally, *El Elyon.* The throne of heaven and of earth is His by divine right.

When we think of ourselves in relation to such an one, how pitiful, how insignificant, we feel! Well might the Psalmist exclaim, "When I consider Thy heavens . . . what is man, that Thou art mindful of him?" (Psa. 8: 3, 4), and St. James observe, "What is your life? It is even a vapour that . . . vanisheth away" (Jas. 4: 14). While that is true, however, it is far from all the truth. God, so high and holy, has created us for His own pleasure and peculiar possession. His delights are with the sons of men. The Most High God is our loving heavenly Father. In Christ, He is our Redeemer and Friend.

The problems and pains of life often harass and grieve us. Amid them all, the child of God is trustful and unafraid, knowing that the Lord Jesus, our Saviour, is *El Elyon.* He knows the way that we take; and through His overruling providence "all things work together for good to them that love God." Our *El Shaddai* is *El Elyon.*

For all that is expressed in this name, in its use in the Old Testament, is true of our Lord Jesus Christ. Because of His obedience to the will of the Father, even unto the death of the Cross, God has highly exalted Him, and given Him the name above every name, that at the name of Jesus every knee should bow. In sharp contrast to Lucifer's arrogant pride and unholy ambition, He has through humility and self-emptying been exalted far above all. Lucifer, through lifting up his heart in pride, has been cast into lowest hell; our Lord Jesus, through stooping in lowliness to the manger and to the Cross, has been seated at the right hand of the majesty on high. Well might St. Paul apply this lesson to us: "Let this mind be in you, which was also in Christ Jesus . . ." (Phil. 2: 5).

He who is exalted is the One who humbled Himself for us men and our salvation. He is the Man Christ Jesus, now glorified in the throne; our great High Priest, and our Advocate. Because He is there, we may come boldly to the throne: for the throne of the heavenly majesty is now a throne of grace. And coming, we shall find grace to help in every time of need.

Gracious—and mighty. *El Shaddai* and *El Elyon*. He is *able to do* exceeding abundantly above all that we ask or think. He is *able to keep* that which we have committed unto Him against that day. He is *able to present* us faultless before the divine majesty with exceeding joy: for the Most High God determined before all ages, through Christ, to show forth His glory—the glory of His grace—eternally in His saints, the redeemed sons of men.

CHAPTER EIGHT

El Olam—The Everlasting God

The same yesterday, today forever—for all generations, yet essentially the same [handwritten annotation]

A NAME of God which occurs only a comparatively few times in the Scriptures, yet is revealing of a wondrous aspect of His character, is *El Olam*, translated in the Authorized Version, "the Everlasting God." Its meaning is somewhat difficult to convey, for the Hebrew word *olam* cannot be expressed in any one English word—it is, indeed, translated in several different ways in the Old Testament, including "everlasting," "evermore," "old," "old time," "ancient time," "beginning of the world," "continuance," and—most frequently of all—"ever." So while "the Everlasting God" catches something of the significance of *El Olam*, it does not fully convey its meaning.

The first use of the divine names, as we have seen, often supplies a clue to their true value. In this case, however, the circumstances do not provide any very clear indication. Abraham, shortly before his testing concerning the offering of Isaac, reproved Abimelech because of the well of water which Abimelech's servants had violently taken away; so they made a covenant at Beer-sheba, and Abraham "planted a grove at Beer-sheba, and called there on the name of the LORD, the Everlasting God" (Gen. 21: 33). It would seem that, with all his knowledge and experience of God, Abraham felt that in committing this matter to Him, he was entering upon another new experience of the riches of His grace, which necessitated the use of yet another name for God. He entrusted his cause to the One who is always available, always cognizant of all the facts, always able to vindicate the trust which His children repose in Him. Or, to use our modern theological terminology, that God is omnipresent, omniscient, and omnipotent.

45

"Change: decay, in all around I see
O thou who changest not, abide with Me."

X =
Changeless
yet
changing
G Heb 13

Now, that is precisely the thought which underlies most of the passages in which this title *El Olam* occurs. In a word, it conveys, not merely that God is "everlasting"—the Eternal God—but that He is, in all the succeeding generations, just what His people need Him to be. *They* change from generation to generation; and their needs change with them. He never changes: He is the eternal, unchangeable Lord; yet He is, in all the changing scenes of life, *exactly what His people need Him to be.* "Thy mercies," said David, "have been ever of old (*olam*)"—Psalm 25: 6; and again, "For the LORD is good; His mercy is from everlasting to everlasting; and His truth endureth to all generations" (Psa. 100: 5); and yet again, "The mercy of the LORD is from everlasting to everlasting upon them that fear Him, and His righteousness unto children's children" (Psa. 103: 17). In these and other passages, "from everlasting to everlasting" could obviously be rendered "from generation to generation."

p45

But a more limited application of the word *olam* is indicated in several passages, in which it is translated "for ever," but with the underlying meaning of "for the entire life-time." The slave who renounced his privilege of going free in the year of jubilee, choosing instead to serve his master perpetually, had his ear bored with an awl, thus binding him to his master's service "for ever" (Exod. 21: 6). Hannah brought her young son Samuel to the tabernacle at Shiloh, "that he may appear there for ever" (1 Sam. 1: 22), that is, for the rest of his life (v. 28). Abraham, in calling upon *El Olam* at Beer-Sheba, may have meant that he looked to God to attest his covenant with Abimelech as long as he should live. And God is indeed our God unto life's last breath.

But far more than either of these suggestions is contained within the name *El Olam*. God is more than the "God of generations" and "age-abiding"—as some translators render the name: He is "from everlasting to everlasting" in all the sweep of that stupendous statement. "From everlasting to everlasting, Thou art God" (Psa. 90: 2). From before all ages, unto all eternity, He is the everlasting I AM.

And He is *our* God. We, who are creatures of an hour, so far
as this earthly life is concerned, are lifted up into the eternal
will and purpose and life of God, in Christ our Lord (Rom.
8: 29, 30; Eph. 1: 4, 5, 11). God foreknew us in Christ "before
the foundation of the world"; our lives are related to His eternal
purposes; and He gives us grace according to the age in which
we live.

It is an absorbing study, outside the scope of our present
purpose, to trace in the Word of God the course of His plan for
the ages. From the few scattered references to the counsels
between the Father and the Son before the world began, in
which the Second Person of the Godhead was set apart as "the
Lamb . . . slain from the foundation of the world," we can
follow the outworking of that divine pre-determination, through
the ordered processes of creation, and the divine dealings with
man, to the supreme act of self-revelation and redeeming grace
in the Incarnation, which ushered in this "day of grace"—and
on, unto the ultimate consummation of all His purposes set
forth in the Book of Revelation.

In earlier generations, God dealt with His people according
to the needs of *their* day; and now, His grace is sufficient for us
in this troubled twentieth century. How very different are our
times and circumstances from those of Abraham, Isaac, and
Jacob! But the same Everlasting God meets our needs as fully
and graciously as He did theirs: and He will do so as long as
life shall last.

How apposite are the words of the apostle: "Now to Him
that is of power to stablish you according to my Gospel, and the
preaching of Jesus Christ . . . according to the commandment of
the Everlasting God, made known to all nations . . ." (Rom.
16: 25, 26). And one last word from Isaiah—"Hast thou not
known? hast thou not heard, that the Everlasting God, the
LORD, the Creator of the ends of the earth, fainteth not, neither
is weary? . . . they that wait upon the LORD shall renew their
strength; they shall mount up with wings as eagles; they shall
run and not be weary; and they shall walk and not faint"
(Isa. 40: 28–31).

CHAPTER NINE

El Roi—"Thou God Seest Me"

Lᴇsᴛ ɪᴛ be thought that the self-revelation of God was made exclusively to and through *men*, it is eminently fitting that one of the most tender of the divine names should have first found expression on the lips of a woman—*El Roi*, "Thou God seest me" (Gen. 16: 13). It was Hagar who thus "called the name of the Lord that spake unto her," and the name was born out of her own experience of grace in her extremity of need. Sarai, having suggested to Abram that he should have a son by Hagar, her Egyptian hand-maid, then turned against the girl and "dealt hardly with her," so that she "fled from her face." Alone in the wilderness, and probably panic-stricken with fear, "the angel of the Lᴏʀᴅ found her," and gave her comfort and counsel.

"Thou God seest me." What an unspeakable relief that realization must have brought to the terror-stricken mind and over-wrought nerves of the fugitive, as she sat by the "fountain of water in the wilderness" and thought upon her plight. She had been goaded by the unkindness of her mistress to run away from the nomadic encampment of Abram; but now that she was alone in this frightful wilderness, where could she go, and what would happen to her? In her great need, "the angel of the Lᴏʀᴅ found her." She herself summed up all that this meant, in the name for God which she was inspired to utter— *El Roi.* God saw—and "to her rescue came." For with God, to see is to act. He does not "see" with the cold eye of unconcerned omniscience; His is the watchful care of a heavenly Father. Thus, when He appeared to Moses in the burning bush He said, "I have surely seen the affliction of My people

48

which are in Egypt . . . and I am come to deliver them"
(Exod. 3: 7, 8).

The literal translation of *El Roi* is "A God of seeing," or "of
vision." There is some dispute between scholars whether this
means that God *sees*, or *permits Himself to be seen*. We may take
the benefit of both translations, for both are true! There is
support for the latter rendering in the fact that the well, beside
which Hagar had this spiritual experience, was given the name
Beer-lahai-roi—"The well of him that liveth and seeth Me," or
"the well of the living seeing," i.e., "the well of continuing to
live after seeing God" (cf. Gen. 32: 30; Exod. 3: 6; Jud. 13:
22). It was considered so awesome a thing to look upon God
with mortal eyes, that death must surely ensue; but God, all-
holy though He be, is a God of grace, and grants the vision of
Himself, not to blight men's lives, but to bless them. "Look
unto Me, and be ye saved, all ye ends of the earth" is a Gospel
note in the Old Testament as well as the New.

There is, however, a profound wealth of comfort, as well as
of arresting challenge, in the thought of the all-seeing eye of
God. He knows us altogether; nothing is hid from the Lord
(Psa. 139: 1, 2). While that is a sobering realization, it is also
wondrously reassuring to His true children—God being such
an One as He is! When, like Hagar, we think we are quite
alone, and in a frightful predicament, "Thou God seest."
"The eye of the LORD is on them that fear Him, upon them that
hope in His mercy" (Psa. 33: 18). He knows, too, all the
inequalities and vicissitudes of life, and will vindicate righteousness and judge iniquity—"The eyes of the Lord are over the
righteous, and His ears are open unto their prayer: but the
face of the Lord is against them that do evil" (1 Pet. 3: 12).
Indeed, the references are legion: we must conclude with one
of especial appeal to many Christians—"I will guide thee with
Mine eye" (Psa. 32: 8). Here, such an intimacy of relationship
and constancy of fellowship with God is suggested, that the
mere glance of His eye is enough to indicate the way in which
He would have us to go. A slightly different thought is conveyed, however, by the more accurate rendering of the Revised

Version—"I will counsel thee with Mine eye upon thee"; but the same wondrous relationship of grace is implied. "My eye shall be on thee, watching and directing thy way" (JFB Commentary).

El Roi. "The well of him that liveth and seeth Me"—yes, *liveth*; for this is life indeed, the only true life: to know God, and behold Him, and obey Him.

CHAPTER TEN

Jehovah-sabaoth—The LORD of Hosts

AVING considered some of the divine titles compounded
with *El*, we come now to the larger group of names in
which *Jehovah* is joined to other words describing specific
aspects of His character and grace. One of the most important
of these, and the most frequently used in Scripture, is *Jehovah-
sabaoth*, "the LORD of hosts." It is a name somewhat similar to
El Elyon, "the Most High God," but with a further unfolding
of the greatness of His power and love toward men.

Again we must remind ourselves that, as in all the composite names of God, the first part has its full measure of
meaning. All that *Jehovah* is, He is as *Jehovah-sabaoth*. Just as
El, in such compound names as *El Elyon*, speaks of His might,
so *Jehovah*, His personal name, expresses His relationship to His
people: He is the God of grace, who has entered into covenant
relationship with them. He it is who is *Jehovah-sabaoth*, the
LORD of hosts.

This name is not used at all in the early books of the Bible.
It first appears in Samuel, and occurs mostly in the utterances
and writings of the prophets.

What, then, does it really mean? We have a foreshadowing of
it in Genesis 32: 2, where Jacob, on his way back to Canaan and
his dreaded meeting with his brother Esau, was confronted by
"the angels of God." And when Jacob saw them, he said,
"This is God's host." So angels are part, at least, of the hosts
of the LORD. David frequently refers to them as such (cf.
Psa. 103: 21; 148: 2).

It would be a mistake, however, to think that the title
Jehovah-sabaoth refers only to the heavenly hosts. For this word
"hosts" is used also concerning Israel. At the very beginnings

51

of their history as a nation, in their deliverance from Egypt, we read, ". . . all the hosts of the LORD went out from the land of Egypt" (Exod. 12: 41), and that term is, from then onwards, frequently applied to them. The title *Jehovah-sabaoth* therefore embraces both the heavenly and earthly hosts of the LORD; and the thought expressed in it is the joining of the heavenly forces with the earthly people of God—the bringing of heavenly power to the aid of His elect.

This is well illustrated in the matchless story of Joshua's meeting with the Stranger before Jericho, whom he accosted with the challenge, "Art thou for us, or for our adversaries?"—to receive the reply, "Nay; but as captain of the host of the LORD am I now come" (Josh. 5: 13, 14). Israel was indeed to battle for the land: but they would not obtain it by their sword and bow—the LORD would give them the victory, through His aid from on high.

It is not surprising, therefore, that although there had been these foreshadowings of it earlier, the name *Jehovah-sabaoth* is first used in the Book of Samuel. At a time when Israel had sunk into weakness and bondage through sinful self-indulgence and apostasy, God was still ready to respond with irresistible might to the faith and loyalty of even a few.

In accord with this, the very first occurrence of the name is in connection with the faith and worship of one godly Israelite. At a time when the nation as a whole was regardless of God, Elkanah "went . . . yearly to worship and to sacrifice unto the LORD of hosts in Shiloh" (1 Sam. 1: 3). Despite the defection of His people, He was "the LORD of hosts"—and that fact is stirringly demonstrated in the following chapters, which tell how, within the lifetime of two men—Samuel (Elkanah's son), and David (whom Samuel anointed to be king)—Israel was raised from defeat and ignominy to the summit of its glory and strength, through the grace and might of *Jehovah-sabaoth*. No wonder this is the characteristic name for God in this book!

He would not countenance, however, any sham or super-stitious "faith"; so that when the Israelites brought the Ark of the Covenant into the field of battle in the name of the LORD of hosts, He allowed it to be captured by the Philistines, and Israel to be discomfited (1 Sam. 4: 4, 10–11). But when a David went against the champion of the Philistines "in the name of the LORD of hosts," He wrought a great deliverance for him and for the nation (1 Sam. 17: 45–53).

The thought expressed in this name, then, is the heavenly aid available to the people of God in their time of need, as they unfeignedly put their trust in *Jehovah-sabaoth*. This was so in the case of Isaiah, distressed by the death of Uzziah—a strong and good king, albeit he was smitten with leprosy for intruding into the duties of the priests. Meditating in the temple, Isaiah "saw the LORD sitting upon a throne" and heard the seraphims cry, "Holy, holy, holy, is the LORD of hosts" (Isa. 6: 3). He it was who gave the prophet His sovereign command and commission to the nation. Much later, Haggai encouraged the remnant who returned to the land after the captivity, with the assurances of the LORD of hosts (Haggai 2: 4–6); and Malachi uttered his stirring challenge, accompanied by its almost limitless promise, in the name of the LORD of hosts—"Bring ye all the tithes into the storehouse . . . and prove Me now herewith, saith the LORD of hosts, if I will not open you the windows of heaven, and pour you out a blessing, that there shall not be room enough to receive it" (Mal. 3: 10).

Jehovah-sabaoth is thus presented to us as the LORD of the heavenly hosts, and the Guardian and Helper of His earthly people. But He is *their* Lord, too: He is *Jehovah* (their God) *sabaoth*. They are part of His hosts. He rules in the armies of heaven and of earth. Indeed, all His creatures are under His command, and must obey His sovereign will—consciously or otherwise; willingly or not. Thus even the armies of the alien were used by Him as a scourge to His own people, when they were rebellious and backsliding. How terrible is the thought of the LORD of hosts fighting *against* His own people—instead of with them—because of their sin! That is the inevitable consequence of waywardness and cherished evil.

While that must be recognized, however, the dominant thought expressed in this name is comforting and reassuring.

There are illimitable resources at the disposal of God on behalf of His people, of which we have but the smallest comprehension. The Bible is reticent concerning the ministry of angels; but we know that they are "ministering spirits, sent forth to minister for them who shall be heirs of salvation." Beyond that, we have little right to speculate.

This we know, however: that during the earthly life of our Lord, angels were His frequent attendants. Angels both foretold and heralded His birth (Luke 1: 26–38; 2: 13, 14); safeguarded Him in infancy (Matt. 2: 13); succoured Him after the Temptation in the wilderness (Matt. 4: 11); strengthened Him in the Garden (Luke 22: 43); proclaimed His resurrection (Matt. 28: 2–7); and will accompany His return (Matt. 16: 27). He declared, in His resurrection triumph, "All power (authority) is given unto Me in heaven and in earth" (Matt. 28: 18). Now, He commands those angels on our behalf. For He is *Jehovah-sabaoth*. And He has promised, "Lo, I am with you alway, even unto the end of the world" (v. 20). Well might we look to Him with unquestioning confidence, in every time of need—

> And ask the aid of heavenly power
> To help us in the evil hour.

Commander-in-chief of the angels—! all men—to serve the purpose of grace.

CHAPTER ELEVEN

Jehovah-jireh—The LORD Will Provide *— a Substitute; Favour; Sacrifice*

ONE OF the most interesting of the titles of God, *Jehovah-jireh*, has captured the imagination of Christian people to an exceptional degree, so that it is one of the best known of the compound names of the LORD. Yet, strictly speaking, it is not used in Scripture as a divine title at all! *Jehovah-jireh* occurs only once in the Old Testament, and then it is the name of a *place* (Gen. 22: 14). But the faith of the people of God has laid hold upon this name, and raised it to the level of a title of God. And truly it is so: for God is *Jehovah-jireh*, and the place so named bore testimony to what He is—and ever will be to those who put their trust in Him.

To many Christian people, the words *Jehovah-jireh* have a special association with the China Inland Mission, which from its earliest days adopted this phrase, and *Ebenezer*, "Hitherto hath the Lord helped us," as its twin mottoes. They regularly appear, in Chinese characters and in English, on the front page of the Mission's magazine; and are inscribed on either side of the portal of the Mission's headquarters in London. The implication of *Jehovah-jireh*, as so used, is that God will provide for the daily needs of those who look to Him in faith. That is undoubtedly a legitimate use of the phrase, since—as a proverb assures us—"the greater includes the lesser"; and St. Paul has laid down the principle, "He that spared not His own Son, but delivered Him up for us all, how shall He not with Him also freely give us all things?" (Rom. 8: 32).

But such provision is not the thought originally expressed in this phrase, *Jehovah-jireh*: it was something far more profound than that. We do well to remind ourselves of the supreme experience of Abraham's life of faith, on Mt. Moriah, and the

55

value it imparted to this name, lest we rob it of its deepest meaning by thinking only of the provision of temporal necessities.

Abraham had come to the happy eventide of his life. The long testing of his faith, concerning the birth of a son, had given place to joy unspeakable in the gift of Isaac. He was at peace in the land where he sojourned: all disputings with his neighbours were ended, and he was prospering remarkably.

Suddenly, in the midst of this tranquil and happy life, came a command from God—a startling, incredible command, to take Isaac to Moriah and offer him there in sacrifice. Yet, incomprehensible as it was that the God whom he had come to know so well and trust so implicitly should require him to sacrifice his son—the son repeatedly promised, and given in fulfilment of that promise—the command was unmistakable. There was only one thing for Abraham to do, and that was to obey. And he proved himself to be indeed a man of faith, by obeying without hesitation. He "arose early in the morning," and set out, with Isaac, for the place which God had appointed.

It is one thing to perform an act of obedience in the first impulse of response to the divine voice, and quite another thing steadfastly to abide by that decision. It is one thing to set out upon a costly enterprise, and quite another thing to see it through to the end. How many there are who, like the Galatians, begin well, but "peter out" (Gal. 5: 7). Abraham was not like that. He had plenty of time for "second thoughts" upon his initial obedience. For three days they journeyed; and all the while he was pondering upon this strange command of God—and to his own perplexities were added the questionings of Isaac.

How easy it would have been to argue himself out of his first impulse of obedience; to persuade himself that he was mistaken, and that God could never have made such a demand! There can be no doubt that Abraham was tempted to do so, for he—like Elijah, centuries later—was "a man of like passions as we are." But instead of yielding to the temptation, he faced the facts squarely and came to the firm conviction that, since God required him to offer Isaac in sacrifice, He was also "able to raise him up, even from the dead"—for the promises He had given concerning Isaac could not fail of fulfilment (Heb. 11: 19).

Now we, looking back upon the scene on Mt. Moriah, can realize more fully than he probably did at the time, all that was involved in that remarkable drama. Some of the profoundest spiritual lessons of the whole of God's dealings with men were given there, in parable and type, for the instruction of all generations. Not only was the faith of Abraham perfected by this supreme act of obedience, but he here learned *the significance of sacrifice*. Until that day, the offering of sacrifice had been to him an act of worship: the appointed means of approach by man to God. Now, he was taught its true, deep significance; and through him, all mankind have learned that most important of lessons.

Isaac was the joy and rejoicing of Abraham's heart. He could see no fault in the lad. Yet God demanded his life, upon the altar. Abraham could not for a moment consider this to be a caprice on the part of God. He had to learn that, whatever Isaac might seem in Abraham's eyes, he was before God a sinner; and "the wages of sin is death." His life was forfeit, and God demanded it. And Abraham did not challenge the justice of that verdict, nor dispute the divine command. By his obedient faith, he both stated and foreshadowed the most wondrous mystery of divine grace.

"God will provide Himself a lamb," he said, in reply to Isaac's questioning—and therein he uttered, perhaps all unconsciously to himself, one of the clearest Old Testament anticipations of the glorious message of John 3: 16. Out of the agony of his bitter distress, in the inexplicable leadings of God, was born a fellowship with the Father in the giving of His Son, more intimate than any other mortal was ever privileged to know.

And so Isaac was bound with cords, and laid upon the altar; the knife was raised, and—the angel of the LORD stayed his hand, with authoritative voice from heaven. "And Abraham lifted up his eyes, and behold behind him a ram caught in a thicket by the horns: and Abraham went and took the ram, and offered him up for a burnt-offering in the stead of his son. And Abraham called the name of that place *Jehovah-jireh*: as it is said unto this day, In the mount of the LORD it shall be seen" (Gen. 22: 13, 14).

Here, in the peerless words of Scripture, we are taught the great truth of substitution; that "God will provide" a lamb to take the place of the guilty sinner; that in virtue of that offering, the one whose life was forfeit might go free. It is so wonderful a picture of the Atonement effected by our Lord upon the Cross, "in the stead of" guilty sinners, that we scarcely need the assurance which our Lord gave—"Abraham rejoiced to see My day; he saw it, and was glad" (John 8: 56).

In his book, *The Titles of Jehovah*, Preb. H. W. Webb-Peploe points out that, in this story, the name for God used in the early part is *Elohim*, while in the latter part, from the command of the angel onward, *Jehovah* is used. He therefore suggests that it was God in His capacity as *Elohim* who demanded the offering of Isaac, while in His capacity as *Jehovah* He provided the substitute. But we cannot agree that these different names of God reveal Him in different "capacities," in this way. As we have seen, *Elohim* is *Jehovah*; and *Jehovah* is *Elohim*. Each name contains something distinctive in its revelation of God: but it is *the same God* who is spoken of by either name—or any other of the many names by which He made Himself more fully known. A fundamental of His character is that He is "without variableness, or shadow of turning" (Jas. 1: 17).

Indeed, one of the most comforting revelations of the whole Word of God is contained within this very fact. For it is the God who condemns our sin, who Himself provides the substitute. Abraham spoke more than he knew when, in reply to Isaac, he said—by the Spirit, albeit unconsciously—"*Elohim* will provide Himself a lamb . . ." And St. Paul declares the same truth when he says, "the wrath of God is revealed from heaven against all ungodliness and unrighteousness of men," but in the Gospel "is the righteousness of God revealed, from faith to faith"

(Rom. 1: 17, 18)—the gift of righteousness, bestowed by God from heaven upon all who trust in the Lord Jesus Christ our Saviour (3: 20, 21).

God has indeed provided "the Lamb of God, which taketh away the sin of the world." The giving of His Son to be our Saviour was more costly and grievous to the Father, than even this experience of Abraham can dimly portray: for the sorrow of Abraham was that of a man, while the Passion of Christ was the sorrow of God—as far beyond our comprehension as the majesty of His Being is beyond our understanding. And Abraham was not required to go to the ultimate length of actually giving his son—though in spirit he did so. But on Calvary our Saviour died: "God so loved the world that He gave His only begotten Son"—*unto death*. Isaac was spared, and the ram substituted, to teach us a great lesson: but the Son of God *is* our Substitute, the Lamb who died "for us men and our salvation."

In the fellowship between Abraham and Isaac in this act of devotion and dedication we have a faint but wonderful picture of fellowship between the Father and the Son in the outworking of our redemption. For Isaac was not—as is usually thought— a mere child, passively submissive to the will of his father: he was a youth in the full flowering of his strength, who must have understood and consented, or he could have resisted so aged a man as Abraham. So, while "God so loved that He gave . . ." it is equally true that "the Son of God loved me, and gave Himself for me."

More even than that: the faith of Abraham reached beyond the length of obedience unto death: he "accounted that God was able to raise him up, even from the dead: *whence also he received him in a figure*" (Heb. 11: 19). And so he entered into an understanding of the purposes and grace of God, who gave His Son unto the death of the Cross, in order that He might bring many sons unto glory; and into a fellowship with the Lord Himself, "Who for the joy that was set before Him endured the cross, despising the shame." He looked beyond, to the glory that should follow.

No wonder *Jehovah-jireh* is a precious name for God, to all who have by faith received the benefits of His atoning grace, in the joyous assurance of sins forgiven, the gift of righteousness, and life everlasting. The Lord has indeed provided the Lamb without blemish and without spot; the Lamb of God, who taketh away the sins of the world. "In the mount of the Lord it shall be seen." On Calvary we witness the love that passeth knowledge; the divine provision for our deepest need; the answer to everything in us that would condemn. The Lord has provided a ransom. Jesus has died, "the Just for the unjust, to bring us to God." The Holy One is our Redeemer, our Righteousness, from faith to faith!

(ii) Ebenezer. Like *Jehovah-jireh*, and certain other titles, *Ebenezer* was a name given to an altar: but in this case the title is not applied to God Himself. Rather is it an expression of gratitude to Him, and public testimony to His grace. The altar was erected by Samuel, to celebrate and commemorate the victory granted by God against the Philistines, after long subjection to them (1 Sam. 7: 12). The Israelites recognized that they had not gained the victory through their own strategy or prowess: it was of the Lord. So with grateful hearts they "raised their Ebenezer." Literally, the word means "The stone of help," but it is rightly regarded as signifying—as the Israelites gladly proclaimed when they erected it—"Hitherto hath the Lord helped us." It was more than an acknowledgment of grace received, however: it was an encouragement for days to come—for past mercies beget confidence in like benefits in present and future time of need. The circumstances and significance of this title have much in common with those of *Jehovah-nissi* (see pp. 67–70).

CHAPTER TWELVE

Jehovah-rapha—The LORD that Healeth

NEW EXPERIENCES of God, on the part of His children, called for new names to express the truth concerning Him which they had learned. Sometimes these new names were ascribed to God by men, as in the case of *Jehovah-jireh*; but others were pronounced by God Himself as part of His progressive self-revelation. Among such names was *Jehovah-rapha*, "The LORD that healeth."

It was not long after their departure from Egypt that Israel met their first testing. They had seen the mighty wonders of God's delivering grace, as they came out of Egypt; then, after passing through the Red Sea, they sang the song of triumph which is recorded in Exodus 15: 1–19, and Miriam, with a timbrel, led the joyous dancing of the women. A three-days' march through the wilderness followed, and they "found no water." By now their water bottles, filled before they left Egypt, were empty, and they were thirsty and apprehensive. It is difficult for us, in our well-watered land, to appreciate the desperate anxiety of such a situation—and the intense relief when a spring of water was found. With what eagerness the people would rush to drink; and with what consternation, if not panic, they would look at one another as they tasted the water and found it bitter!

This was the first of the many vicissitudes of the wilderness journey, allowed by God in order to test His people. "There," says the Word, "He proved them" (Exod. 15: 25). And for the first of the many times in their wanderings, they "murmured against Moses" and demanded querulously, "What shall we drink?" Behind their complaint, of course, was fear—an unspoken dread of death for lack of water. This was natural enough: yet how unreasonable, since God was with them! If only they had stopped to think, they must have realized that He who had done so much for them—whose power they had witnessed in such miraculous fashion—would not let them perish now, of thirst. But they did not think: they saw before them what seemed to be a calamitous plight, and they panicked. And who feels qualified to blame them? Most of us have behaved precisely like that, in circumstances which have tested our faith. It is so much easier to be appalled by "hard facts" than to be strong and steadfast in faith, assured that the God of the impossible will undertake for us.

God did not deal with them according to their deserving, however: He who does not break the bruised reed gave them a speedy proof of His presence with them, and His power to meet their every need. He "showed Moses a tree, which when he had cast into the waters, the waters were made sweet." There have been many speculations whether or not the tree had medicinal properties: but obviously the purpose of the casting of the tree into the water was to fasten the attention of the people upon the fact that *God* was *healing* the waters. It was a miracle. He who had brought them out of Egypt, now provided for their urgent need in the wilderness. Their fear was turned into rejoicing. God had intervened once more on their behalf.

In that moment of a new experience of God, they were challenged to trust and obey Him henceforward, without demur. "There He made for them a statute and an ordinance . . . and said, If thou wilt diligently hearken unto the voice of the LORD thy God . . . I will put none of these diseases upon thee, which I have brought upon the Egyptians: for I am the LORD that healeth thee (*Jehovah-rapha*)."

Now, this wondrous promise obviously related to physical health and well-being; but equally obviously it is linked with the "healing" of the water, by the casting in of a tree, which most Bible students agree to be an "enacted parable" of spiritual healing, through the Cross.

As to its physical aspect, Moses himself was the first to claim the promise contained in this name, when he pleaded with God on behalf of Miriam, after she had been stricken with leprosy—"Heal her now, O God, I beseech Thee" (Num. 12: 13). And Miriam proved Him to be indeed *Jehovah-rapha.* The promise was abundantly fulfilled, too, in the experience of all the people, as Moses implied in his farewell speech when they stood at the threshold of the promised land—"Thy raiment waxed not old upon thee, *neither did thy foot swell,* these forty years" (Deut. 8: 4). Nor was the promise confined to the days of their wandering: physical well-being was a covenant blessing upon those who observed the conditions, throughout all Old Testament times. David said, "O LORD, I cried unto Thee, and Thou hast healed me" (Psa. 30: 2); "the LORD . . . who healeth all thy diseases" (Psa. 103: 3); "He sent His word, and healed them" (Psa. 107: 20). It has always been a great comfort to the people of God to know that He who made us cares for us, and graciously meets the needs even of our physical frame.

Of the many occasions on which this word *rapha* is used in the Old Testament, however, only comparatively few have to do with physical health. David sounded a deeper note when he wrote, "He healeth the broken in heart, and bindeth up their wounds" (Psa. 147: 3). And to all except hypochondriacs, this is a far more important matter. The aches and afflictions of the heart are more grievous than the most painful bodily ills. The God who can comfort and strengthen in *such* time of need, is truly *Jehovah-rapha.* How much we could say upon this aspect of His grace—from the Word, and personal experience. Let us each remind ourselves of His goodness, as the Psalmist did, and give Him the thanks which are His due.

But David had something still further to say upon this theme: physical illness directed his thoughts to the more serious malady of the soul. First came the assurance, concerning the godly, when on "the bed of languishing"—"Thou wilt make all his bed in his sickness" (Psa. 41: 3). Then followed the prayer, hand-in-hand with confession, "LORD, be merciful unto me: *heal my soul;* for I have sinned against Thee" (v. 4). That touches upon man's deepest need, and the supreme grace of *Jehovah-rapha* to meet it.

The prophets re-echo this note, again and again. Isaiah, after uttering warnings of divine judgment upon the nation because of sin, foretold also the time when God would "heal the stroke of their wound" (30: 26; 57: 19). Jeremiah complained of the false prophets who "healed also the hurt . . . of My people slightly" (6: 14; 8: 11), and looked forward, like Isaiah, to the day when the LORD would say, "I will restore health unto thee, and I will heal thee of thy wounds" (30: 17). And the One whom he knew to be the nation's only Physician, he sought concerning his personal need—"Heal me, O LORD, and I shall be healed; save me, and I shall be saved" (17: 14). Hosea, a contemporary of Isaiah, records the superficial repentance of Ephraim, "Come, let us return unto the LORD: for He hath torn, and He will heal us" (6: 1), and after exposing the shallowness of this, and stressing the need for true repentance, gives the assurance from God—"I will heal their backsliding, I will love them freely" (14: 4).

Here are promises to cover the whole range of need of His people—for spirit, soul, and body. Whatever their condition might be, His grace is available to those who fulfil the conditions. Those conditions are simple and explicit: "If thou wilt diligently hearken to the voice of the LORD thy God, and wilt do that which is right in His sight . . ." (Exod. 15: 26). In a word, trust and obey.

That was God's pledge under the old covenant. What is its relevance to us to-day? "All the promises of God in Him [our Lord Jesus Christ] are yea, and in Him Amen" (2 Cor. 1: 20). Jesus is *Jehovah-rapha* to His people. One of His best-loved titles is "the Great Physician." He began His earthly ministry by quoting from Isaiah, "The Spirit of the Lord is upon Me . . . to heal the broken-hearted, to preach deliverance to the captives, and recovering of sight to the blind . . ." (Luke 4: 18). Among the most moving scenes in the Gospel story are those which depict Him surrounded by sick and impotent folk, "and He healed them all" (Matt. 12: 15; 14: 14, etc.).

Although He had compassion on all in physical distress, however, and by His miracles of healing showed forth the tender
mercy and wondrous power of God, it was not merely to heal
sick bodies that He came—as some preachers and social workers
would seem to imply. John stresses, in his Gospel, that the
miracles were "signs"—parables in the physical realm of what
He had come to do in the spiritual realm. And He Himself
clearly stated this on at least one occasion: "That ye may know
that the Son of Man hath power on earth to forgive sins (then
saith He to the sick of the palsy), Arise take up thy bed . . ."
(Matt. 9: 6). The forgiveness of sins, and the life in fellowship
with God which results from this transforming experience, is
His supreme concern for men.

"His touch has still its ancient power." Many a story of
divine healing can be told to-day. The Lord of heaven and earth
cares for us, His children—for these bodies, which are temples
of His Spirit. But we are not *promised* physical health and well-
being. Indeed, to very many true saints—in the New Testament meaning of that word—these are denied. St. Paul, who
healed many in the name of the Lord, prayed the Lord thrice
concerning his own "thorn in the flesh," and received the reply
"My grace is sufficient for thee: for My strength is made perfect
in weakness" (2 Cor. 12: 9).

The promise contained within this name, *Jehovah-rapha*, is for
us, then, the spiritual counterpart of the temporal blessings
assured to Israel of old. It is for *fullness of health*, spiritually, in
our earthly pilgrimage: in Christ we are made, and kept,
"every whit whole." "I am the Lord which healeth *thee*."
Together with that glad assurance, is the guarantee of "living
water." He sustains the new life He imparts. Christ is our
sufficiency, as well as our sanctifier. He is so, through the
Cross. As we "know Him . . . and the fellowship of His
sufferings, being made conformable unto His death" (Phil.
3: 10), we experience the joy and peace which "none
but His loved ones know." The fountains of life are "healed";
all experiences and vicissitudes are "made sweet," for "all
things work together for good to them that love God . . ."

(Rom. 8: 28). Our life becomes a walk with the Crucified, *Jehovah-rapha.*

> The Cross: it takes our guilt away;
>   It holds the fainting spirit up;
> It cheers with hope the gloomy day,   *1a*
>   And sweetens ev'ry bitter cup.

May we be sure that the promises are ours? If we keep the conditions! "If thou wilt hearken . . . and do . . ." Trust and obey!

CHAPTER THIRTEEN

Jehovah-nissi—The LORD my Banner

THE CHILDREN of Israel had not travelled far, in their journey from Egypt to the promised land, before they had to engage in battle with Amalek. The strife was not of their seeking: they were attacked, and had to fight or perish. They were unprepared and ill-equipped: but Moses encouraged them with the assurance that he would stand on the top of the hill "with the rod of God in mine hand"—the token of God's bounteous grace and power in the past, in the deliverance from Egypt, the passage through the Red Sea, and the provision of water from the rock. With that rod held aloft in the sight of all the people, to remind them "from whence cometh their help," Moses interceded with God on behalf of the armies of Israel. And God gave them the victory (Exod. 17: 8-16).

The fight was long and severe, however. Often the outcome seemed doubtful, as the fortunes of battle swayed to and fro—until Moses observed that this movement backwards and forwards coincided with his periods of prayer. "When Moses held up his hand . . . Israel prevailed: and when he let down his hand, Amalek prevailed" (v. 11). But Moses could not maintain the posture of prayer those days—with hands upraised—indefinitely. His "hands were heavy"; so Aaron and Hur supported them, one on either side, "and his hands were steady until the going down of the sun." As a result, "Joshua discomfited Amalek and his people with the edge of the sword."

In celebration of this victory, and as a memorial of their deliverance, "Moses built an altar, and called the name of it *Jehovah-nissi*"—which means, "the LORD is my banner." Like *Jehovah-jireh*, this new title of God was not directly ascribed to

Him, but was given as the name of a place—or rather, of an altar, which also served as a memorial stone.

This name appears in Scripture in this one text alone; but the thought expressed in it occurs repeatedly, on the lips of psalmists and prophets. The Hebrew word *nes*, from which *nissi* is derived, is translated "ensign" and "standard," as well as "banner." David said, "Thou hast given a banner to them that fear Thee" (Psa. 60: 4); and Isaiah uttered the ringing challenge, "Lift up a standard for the people" (Isa. 62: 10). Jeremiah, however, expressed another aspect of the matter, when he told of the sorrow of God in being obliged to send the banners of enemy armies into their land, as a chastisement for their sin—"How long shall I see the standard and hear the sound of the trumpet?" (Jer. 4: 21).

This title of God, then, is associated with the *warfare* of His people. And all must engage in conflict sooner or later: not because He wants them to be aggressive, but because there are enemies which assail them. God could, of course, discomfit all these adversaries and deliver His people, by direct intervention from heaven—as He did again and again for Israel. But that is not usually His way. He ordained that Israel should fight—not in their own strength alone, but relying upon His overruling grace. They were to fight with all their might, but knowing all the while that "the battle is the Lord's," and that He would give them the victory. It would be no mock battle: they would have to exert their utmost strength and resolution; but of the issue there would be no doubt. They would have the satisfaction of conquering; yet they would know also that the victory was from the Lord.

Now, "all these things happened unto them for ensamples: and they are written for our admonition" (1 Cor. 10: 11). Their experiences in everyday life are "types" of the spiritual situations and conditions we are called upon to meet. And conflict is an inevitable aspect of Christian life. There are some children of God who seem to go through life calmly and without trial or storm. They are few: and if we knew all the story of their lives, we should probably find that they have not escaped

the noise and surge of battle, despite appearances to the contrary. St. Paul, in likening the Christian to a soldier, was using
no mere metaphor: nor was his frequent use of the terminology
of warfare merely pictorial.

There are "principalities and powers" of evil, which assail
the Christian (Eph. 6: 12). There is also—and we are even
more frequently conscious of this—an enemy within ourselves:
for Amalek, descendants of Esau, represent the "flesh" which
is hostile to the Spirit (Gal. 5: 17); the "old man" which strives
against the "new man" (Eph. 4: 22-24). If we do not battle,
we inevitably are subdued. Nor is the conflict a mere skirmish:
the fight demands "blood and sweat and tears." But the battle
is the Lord's! He has, on the Cross, triumphed gloriously over
His adversaries and ours (Col. 2: 15); and He makes that
victory effective in our experience (Rom. 8: 1-4). Like the
psalmist we say, "We will rejoice in Thy salvation, and in the
name of our God we will set up our banners" (Psa. 20: 5). He
does not subdue our enemies for us—we must do that. But we,
of ourselves, *cannot* do it! Nor could Israel conquer Amalek:
nevertheless they did! So may we. But it will not be by our
own strength or staying-power: the victory, like the battle, is
the Lord's. Yet, in the wonder of His grace, it will be *our victory
too*. And we shall confess, humbly and gratefully, "The Lord
is my banner."

Three lessons concerning spiritual warfare are paramount in
the story from Exodus. Firstly, we learn that we must "fight
the good fight with all our might," yet conscious of our utter
dependence upon the Lord. That leads to the second point—
that prayer and victory go hand-in-hand. Yet, while the up-
holding of the hands of Moses is often regarded as a type of
prevailing intercessory prayer—and rightly so—our confidence
must be, not in prayer, but in the Lord. And thirdly: surely
the supreme lesson which God desired the people to learn—
and to learn, once for all, in this first battle of their experience
—was that reliance upon God must be sustained to the end.
It is not enough to commit the matter perfunctorily to God,
and then forget that the issue is dependent upon Him. The

uplifted hands of Moses symbolized faith in God, unwavering throughout the hazards of battle. Such faith will express itself in prayer, of course, but the important lesson to learn is that "deliverance is of the Lord"—which is the literal rendering of Psalm 3: 8, "salvation belongeth unto the Lord."

In the moment of their victory, Israel worshipped. "Moses erected an altar." That place of sacrifice became an abiding memorial, a perpetual reminder of God's goodness. In future battles, Israel remembered *Jehovah-nissi*. In any hour of need, it is strengthening indeed to recall His mercies in times past. Sometimes memorial stones bear the words: "To the glory of God, and in commemoration of——" some event in which His grace was manifest. We all should have our "altars" bearing the glad testimony, *Jehovah-nissi*. They will stand us in good stead in future days of testing.

> His grace in times past forbids me to think
> He'll leave me at last in trouble to sink.

Finally, Moses in the mount is a clear Old Testament fore-shadowing of our Lord Jesus Christ, our Intercessor and Commander on high; the Captain of our salvation. It is when "looking unto Jesus" that we shall prevail. Isaiah declared that "When the enemy shall come in like a flood, the Spirit of the LORD shall lift up a standard against him" (Isa. 59: 19). And to make quite clear that the "standard" is Christ Himself, the prophet says, "In that day there shall be a root out of Jesse, which shall stand for an ensign (*nes*) of the people; to it [or rather, *Him*] shall the Gentiles seek . . ." (Isa. 11: 10).

Truly the battle is the Lord's. He has gained the victory, and makes His triumph ours (2 Cor. 2: 14). For Jesus, in whom all the promises contained in these Old Testament names of God are Yea and Amen, is *Jehovah-nissi*, the Lord *our* banner. Weak, insufficient in ourselves, we are yet "more than conquerors through Him that loved us" (Rom. 8: 37).

CHAPTER FOURTEEN

Jehovah-m'qaddishkhem—
The LORD that Sanctifieth

ERHAPS the least familiar of the Old Testament titles of
God, to English-speaking readers of the Bible, is *Jehovah-m'qaddishkhem*, "the LORD that sanctifieth," because it is
not transliterated in our versions, either in the text or margin,
as several other of the divine titles are, such as *Jehovah-jireh*,
Jehovah-nissi, etc. It is, nevertheless, one of the most important
of the names of God, in the abiding value of the teaching it
epitomizes; and it is quite frequently used in Scripture. It is
closely related to *Jehovah-tsidkenu*, "the LORD our righteousness"
(see p. 85).

Its first appearance is in Exodus 31: 13, in connection with
the reiterated command concerning the observance of the
Sabbath. Now the law regarding the Sabbath had been given
before this (Exod. 20: 8–11), but it was repeated when God
gave Moses instructions for the preparation of the tabernacle.
It has been suggested that those engaged in the sacred task of
preparing the sanctuary of the LORD might possibly regard their
work as divine service which they were justified in continuing
on the Sabbath; and so Jehovah made clear that even this
work was subject to the law of the Sabbath—"Verily My Sab-
baths ye shall keep: for it is a sign between Me and you
throughout your generations; that ye may know that I am the
LORD that doth sanctify you."

The Sabbath was God's gracious gift to man: all history
testifies to the inestimable value of it, to spirit, mind, and body.
History also testifies, alas, to the difficulty men find in observing
the Sabbath aright. It was not intended primarily to provide
rest and refreshment: that is secondary. The supreme purpose

71

of the Sabbath is to establish God's claim upon the lives of His people. The one day in seven set apart for worship and spiritual service, rightly observed, would inevitably lead to a true knowledge of God and fellowship with Him. It is absolutely fundamental to a right relationship with God: that is why the law concerning it is so explicit and uncompromising. For the nation, and every individual within it, the full realization of their inheritance as the covenant people of God was dependent upon a strict observance of the Sabbath: for according to this, would be their love and loyalty to Him.

To keep one day in seven really holy, however, is a standard few can attain. Men are lovers of self rather than of God; and even the zealously religious would rather be busy in what they consider to be God's service, than quietly waiting upon Him, in worship and devotion. To meet this deficiency, this consequence of the Fall in human nature, God gave the promise contained within this name: "I am the LORD that doth sanctify you." What He demands, He will provide. He will give them the desire and enablement to obey, if only there is a true responsiveness to His will on their part. That is one of the most glorious truths of divine revelation, repeated in many different ways and contexts, in both the Old Testament and the New. It is the thought underlying the use of this name of God, in its every appearance in the Bible.

As we would expect, *Jehovah m'qaddishkhem* is found several times in Leviticus, where the law of God is set forth in detail, in its application to the everyday conduct of His people. "Sanctify yourselves . . . for I am the LORD which sanctify you" runs like a refrain through the closing chapters of the book (20: 7, 8; 21: 8, 15, 23; 22: 9, 16, 32). Here, the twofold activity, human and divine, is most clearly stated. "Sanctify yourselves," God commands; and then, because that is impossible to unaided man, He goes on to tell of the divine grace available to meet the need: "I am the LORD which sanctify you."

The word "sanctify" has two distinct meanings in Scripture. It is applied to persons and things set apart for holy service, as the priests were, and also the furnishings of the tabernacle and temple (Exod. 28: 41; 29: 36, 37, 44; 40: 10, 11, etc.). In relation to people, however, the word relates also to *character*: they are to be worthy of that "set-apartness." This true sanctification of the whole of life was required not only of the priests, but also the entire nation, since all were His covenant, sanctified people. So from its earliest appearance, this name for God, *Jehovah-m'qaddishkhem*, sets forth the highest standard of His requirements in His elect—conformity to His own holiness.

How impossible a standard! Yet He requires it, and cannot be satisfied with anything less. His own character demands it —as the reference to His holiness in almost every repetition of the command, "sanctify yourselves," emphasizes: "For I the LORD which sanctify you, am holy." But He does not merely issue an edict, as one aloof and inexorable: He is *Jehovah*, the God of covenant grace, who dwells among His people, *to sanctify them*. He will "work in them both to will and to do of His good pleasure" (Phil. 2: 13). Yet not as an irresistible force carrying them along willy-nilly. His sanctifying power, like all His enabling grace, operates in and through the responsive heart and dedicated will. "Sanctify yourselves." The power available will become effectual only in the exertion of earnest endeavour.

These great truths, first expressed so early in Israel's history, reach their full exposition in the New Testament. "This is the will of God," St. Paul declares, "even your sanctification" (1 Thess. 4: 3). The word "sanctification" has an enriched, and yet more concise, meaning in the New Testament than in the Old, as the full wonder of the "high calling of God" in Christ is made known: that the saints should be conformed to the very image of their Lord. So the challenge is issued again and again: "Be ye holy (sanctify yourselves) in all manner of conversation" (1 Pet. 1: 15); "Present your bodies a living sacrifice, holy, acceptable unto God" (Rom. 12: 1); "lifting up holy hands . . ." (1 Tim. 2: 8). We can no more be holy, however, than Israel could. But the impossible is possible, for "I am the LORD which doth sanctify you."

In the fuller light of the New Testament, we realize this transforming work of sanctification to be effected by each of the three Persons of the Triune God: we are "sanctified by God the Father" (Jude 1); by Christ, "who of God is made unto us . . . sanctification" (1 Cor. 1: 30; cf. Heb. 10: 10; 13: 12); and through the Spirit (1 Pet. 1: 2). God, in the totality of His Being, is active in the sanctification of His people.

The teaching of the entire Bible on this great subject is gathered up in the name *Jehovah-m'qaddishkhem*. It is not our present purpose to expound the doctrine of sanctification, but to stress the cardinal facts indicated in this name: that personal sanctification is our responsibility, yet God's; our work, yet God's. We may be holy if we will sanctify ourselves: yet all our sanctification will be the gracious result of God working in us both to will and to do of His good pleasure. The secret lies in two words: strive, and trust.

CHAPTER FIFTEEN

Jehovah-shalom—The LORD Send Peace

G OD DELIGHTS to choose for His service those who consider themselves unequal to such a calling. Gideon was one of these: and his diffidence led to an experience out of which was born a most reassuring new name for God—*Jehovah-shalom*, "the LORD send peace" (Judges 6: 24).

It seemed incredible to Gideon, a young man of lowly family and humble disposition, that the stirring, challenging words of the stranger could be true. He had been threshing wheat in a quiet spot where he hoped he would not be discovered by the Midianite oppressors, lest they should steal the grain he had threshed. Smarting under a keen realization of the hardship and indignity his people were suffering, he yet had no thought that *he* might deliver them from the cursed yoke. When the stranger assured him that he was chosen of the LORD for this task, he could scarcely believe it: yet the word of the Angel of Jehovah was so authoritative that he could not dismiss it altogether. Who was this stranger, however, bringing this extraordinary message, and speaking as if he were Jehovah Himself? In his perplexity, Gideon determined to put the matter to the test. So he asked the stranger to wait while he prepared a meal—the customary courtesy of hospitality in the East. But the stranger had made such an impression on the mind of Gideon that the word he used was "meat offering"; and what he prepared might equally well be a meal for a man, or an offering to God. By what the stranger did with this, Gideon thought, he would learn who he was. So he brought his "present," and was commanded to place it on a wall. Then the stranger touched it with his staff, and flames came out of the wall and devoured the offering; and the stranger "departed out of his sight."

Immediately Gideon was stricken with fear. His doubt as to the identity of the stranger was resolved: he could be no other than "an angel of the LORD"—in fact, He was *the* "Angel of *Jehovah*," the pre-incarnate Lord Jesus Christ. Gideon realized at once that his doubts, and the test he had carried out, might well be deemed unpardonable presumption. "Alas, O Lord GOD!" he cried, "for because I have seen an angel of the LORD face to face" (Judges 6: 22). But swiftly came the divine reassurance: "Peace be unto thee: fear not: thou shalt not die." Then Gideon built an altar there unto the LORD, and called it *Jehovah-shalom* (v. 24). This, then, is yet another name for God associated with an altar.

"The LORD send (or, giveth) peace" is clearly Gideon's grateful acknowledgement of the grace bestowed upon him in the LORD's words, "Peace be unto thee." More than that: his altar, with its name *Jehovah-shalom*, was the expression of his confidence for the future, on the basis of the character of God as he had come to know it through his experience. God, who had given peace, would give it again. As Gideon faced the responsibility to which he had been called—to be leader of the nation in battle—he did so in the assurance that the end would be victory and peace. For the God in whom he trusted was *Jehovah-shalom*. It is one of the most comforting of all truths concerning God, that He is the unchangeable LORD, the same yesterday, and to-day, and for ever (Heb. 13: 8). What we have proved Him to be in times past, we may trust Him to be in days to come. He who had spoken the word of peace to His terror-stricken servant, would also "send peace" to the nation.

That is as true for us to-day as it was for Gideon. And how timely a message this is: for our need of peace in both our personal relationship with God and in the affairs of the world, is as great as was his, so long ago. Like him, we have perhaps doubted whether the voice of God were really His, or not; whether the commands of God were after all only the wishes

and thoughts of men. Then, when we come unmistakably face
to face with God, we tremble, as prophets and seers and millions
of lesser men have done through all the ages, at their first
conscious encounter with the Almighty. When God, and His
claim upon our lives, become a living reality, who of His
creatures does not exclaim, "Woe is me, for I am undone!"
And to all such, as to Gideon, comes the reply of grace, "Peace
be unto thee": for never yet did a soul bow in humility and
contrition before God, without receiving pardon and quicken-
ing grace. And at the word "Peace be unto thee" the heart
is immediately filled with peace: for this is not a mere reassurance, but a creative word—He *giveth* peace.

That word is spoken, now, of course, in Christ. As with other
of these Old Testament names, the ultimate fulfilment of all
that *Jehovah-shalom* expresses, is in our Lord Jesus Christ. He
is our peace (Eph. 2: 14). Under the very shadow of the Cross
He gave, not only to the Twelve, but also to His Church through
them, His bequest of peace (John 14: 27).

Peace is a characteristic word of God to His people, in both
the Old Testament and the New. In a troubled and trouble-
some world, He is the one Source of peace. Yet His promise is
not in accord with our first thoughts upon the matter. Most
people probably relate the word "peace" to earthly circumstances; and indeed we are encouraged to pray for the powers-
that-be, in order that "we may lead a quiet and peaceable
life" (1 Tim. 2: 2). But the Word of God clearly declares what
all history demonstrates, that such peace is the exception rather
than the rule. Our Lord explicitly warned His followers that
"in the world ye shall have tribulation" (John 16: 33). Why
is this? The answer is not always apparent, and we must wait
for it in faith, until we see the events of life—as He does—in
the light of eternity. But this at least we know: that trouble is
often a blessing in disguise. We are so constituted that all too
readily even Christian people become fully satisfied with
worldly peace and prosperity, and forget the One who gave
them. Trouble often drives people to God, and thereby leads
to the secret of true peace. For the peace which this world gives

is deceptive: it tends to lull the spirit to sleep—only to discover too late that it has failed to seek and find peace with God, for eternity. Blessed indeed is the dis-peace which leads to the discovery of the peace of God.

"In the world . . . tribulation," said our Lord; but "in Me . . . peace." A life encompassed in peace, no matter what might happen in the world—that is the inestimable gift of God in Christ. In Him we have peace with God (Rom. 5: 1); the peace which comes with the knowledge of sins forgiven, and reconciliation unto the Father. This was the key-note of apostolic preaching (Acts 10: 36; Eph. 6: 15). Flowing from that, follows the peace of assurance concerning all the affairs and circumstances of life. Not that everything will be made smooth and pleasant; but in every condition and vicissitude "the peace of God, which passeth all understanding, shall keep your hearts and minds through Christ Jesus" (Phil. 4: 7).

Our Lord's words concerning His gift of peace, spoken in the Upper Room, utterly perplexed His disciples. The very foundations of life were being shaken, and evil seemed to be triumphing over good. But after the Resurrection of Christ, they realized that what they had thought to be calamity was the greatest victory of divine grace that even God Himself could conceive: for in the Cross He was redeeming sinful men. Instead of the wicked will of wicked men prevailing over the good purposes of the Lord, He was in command all the time, giving His life a ransom for sinners. Thus the disciples learned that events are not necessarily what they seem to be.

> Ill that He blesses is our good,
> And unblest good is ill;
> And all is right that seems most wrong
> If it be His sweet will.

Our Lord had given an illustration of this, when He stilled the storm on the lake. Doubtless these fishermen had weathered many a storm on Galilee: like most sailors, they rather enjoyed pitting their skill against the elements, and derived deep satisfaction from battling successfully against wind and wave. So most people face the challenge of life with high courage and unquestioning confidence. This storm, however, was unlike any they had ever before encountered: there is a suggestion in the Gospel narrative that it was satanic in origin. However that may be, the disciples realized that, good sailors though they were, this storm was too much for them. The boat was filling with water, and in panic they cried to the Lord, "Master, carest Thou not that we perish?" (Mark 4: 38). He straightway arose, and rebuked the wind and the sea, saying, "Peace, be still." And the wind ceased, and there was a great calm (v. 39). He rebuked them too, saying, "Why are ye so fearful? How is it that ye have no faith?" And their hearts were filled with that sense of awe of which we have spoken, as they realized that the One they knew so well was more than man— "and they feared exceedingly, and said one to another, What manner of man is this, that even the wind and the sea obey Him?" (v. 41).

His stilling of the waves was symbolic of what He is able to do in all the storms of life, and of what He does oft-times for His distressed people. But the point of the story lies in the fact, not that He is able to rebuke and quieten the storm, but that *with Him in the vessel*, His disciples should be calm and unafraid, no matter how the wind might roar and the waves threaten to overwhelm. "Why are ye so fearful?" There is something more precious than calm of situation or circumstance, and that is *faith*. "How is it that ye have no faith?" He asked, reproachfully, disappointedly.

The disciples learned that lesson, and that secret. Those who had been so distressed before Calvary, were calm and joyful afterwards—even in sufferings and persecutions, "rejoicing that they were counted worthy to suffer shame for His name" (Acts 5: 41). They knew indeed His gift of peace; and they counted it far better than any ease and comfort of circumstance. Peace with God had led them into the peace of God; and they knew that He would "ordain peace" for them (Isa. 26: 12) even in seeming vicissitudes, for *all things work together for good to them that love God.* In fellowship with the Prince of peace, His peace which passes all understanding garrisons both heart and mind (see p. 107). "Peace I leave with you, My peace I give unto you: not as the world giveth, give I unto you. Let not your heart be troubled, neither let it be afraid."

CHAPTER SIXTEEN *Ps 23*

Jehovah-rohi—The LORD is my Shepherd

IF ASKED what is their favourite psalm, the majority of people would unhesitatingly reply, "The twenty-third!" Certainly the metaphor of the shepherd presents one of the most winsome of the Biblical word-pictures of God. It appeals as strongly to city-dwellers—even those who have never seen a shepherd among his sheep—as to country folk. That is because it expresses in graphic form a relationship with God for which the heart, albeit unconsciously, yearns. We are created beings, dependent for all our needs upon the mercy and grace of Him who made us. Together with this deep-seated awareness of dependence is a capacity for fellowship with God, which nothing else can satisfy. "The LORD is my shepherd" perfectly expresses the relationship which meets this twofold condition and capacity.

David was a "born shepherd," and Psalm 23 flowed out from the deepest instincts of his heart, as well as from his practical experience. Even when he became king, he thought of himself as the "shepherd" of his people: that is why he was *so may* so good a king. He retained the shepherd-heart; and often, *I as* surely, his thoughts went back to his youthful days, and he *pastor.* almost longed to be out on the hills of Bethlehem again, with his sheep. Then, as he meditated, he realized that all he had sought to be to his sheep, and more, the LORD was to him. So he wrote *Jehovah-rohi*, "the LORD is my Shepherd . . ." He had *Ps 23* cared for his sheep, anticipating their needs and watching over them with kindly concern; he had protected them from danger, even at peril of his life when he slew a lion and a bear; he had led them when necessary to fresh pastures—and though the journey might be arduous and the road rough, he had guided

81

and tended them through all the hazards of the way. In like manner the LORD was with him, caring, leading, providing.

The Psalm, as Dr. Graham Scroggie points out, embraces all the circumstances and conditions of life: the tranquil and the tempestuous; days of testing and of triumph; need and bounteous provision; joy and sorrow—in all, "Thou art with me." The sevenfold testimony, "He maketh . . . leadeth . . . restoreth . . . guideth . . . goeth with . . . preparest . . . anointest . . ." declares the *completeness* of the care of God for His own.

The metaphor of the shepherd is first found in Scripture in the words of Jacob when blessing Joseph, before he died. Looking back upon his long life, with all its varied experiences of happiness and sorrow, penury and prosperity, pettiness and magnanimity—so like the lives of most of us—he said: "God, before whom my fathers Abraham and Isaac did walk, the God which *shepherded* me all my life long . . ." (Gen. 48: 15). This was the most eloquent word which Jacob—a shepherd, like David long afterward—could use. It is indeed a moving picture of the aged patriarch bearing his testimony to the unfailing goodness of God.

The analogy of the shepherd and his sheep is used by several of the prophets regarding the relationship between God and His people (Jer. 31: 10; Ezek. 34: 23; Amos 3: 12. Cf. Zech. 10: 2). It is a vivid metaphor, emphasizing that we, like sheep, are so needy and foolish; while He is so great and good. Isaiah carries the imagery a step further when he says, "All we like sheep have gone astray; we have turned every one to his own way . . ." (53: 6). We must link with this the great Messianic prophecy in Isaiah 40—"He shall feed His flock like a shepherd: He shall gather the lambs with His arm, and carry them in His bosom, and shall gently lead those that are with young" (v. 11). That leads us, in one step, to Christ, "the good Shepherd," in whom all the Old Testament types and prophecies are fulfilled.

That this figure of speech was often in the mind of our Lord, and that He claimed to be the fulfilment of it, is apparent from the frequency of His use of it (Matt. 12: 11; 26: 31. Cf. 18: 12; 25: 32, etc.). The evangelists also, in complete sympathy and understanding of His Person and mission—by the illumination of the Spirit—write of Him as having compassion on the multitude, because they were as sheep without a shepherd (Matt. 9: 36). When sending out the Twelve, He commanded them to go to "the lost sheep of the house of Israel" (Matt. 10: 6). Then in the discourse in John 10, He set forth His teaching and claims in explicit detail.

This chapter is the New Testament counterpart of Psalm 23. Its opening verses, however, refer to the religious leaders in Israel who, instead of "shepherding" those for whom they should have cared, regarded their position merely as a means to personal prestige, authority, and enrichment. In contrast, our Lord described the relationship between Himself and His "own sheep" (v. 4), who know His voice. They become His sheep (a) because He "giveth His life" for them; and (b) because they enter His fold through Him, the door. The first of these two conditions embraces all men: for He died for the sins of the world. Only those who "enter in," however, by personal faith in Him as Saviour, are "saved" (v. 9). To all such He is the Good Shepherd indeed (see p. 152). We can sing Psalm 23 with an even deeper understanding of the riches of its significance, than David who wrote it.

With all the comfort which this brings regarding the everyday experiences and cares of life, there is a deeper note in the Psalm. He who watches over us, and provides for our temporal well-being, will also "shepherd" us concerning all the needs of our spiritual being. Something of what this "shepherding" means is expressed by the writer of the Epistle to the Hebrews. In his majestic doxology he says: "Now the God of peace, that brought again from the dead our Lord Jesus, that great shepherd of the sheep . . . make you perfect in every good work to do His will . . ." (13: 20). What more comprehensive prayer could be uttered than that—"make you perfect to do His will"? It is possible of fulfilment, however, through the grace of God in our Lord Jesus, "the great shepherd of the sheep." With

Him to guide and strengthen, we may be led into "all the fullness of God" (Eph. 3: 19).

There is one further thought, in both Testaments, concerning the Lord as our Shepherd. St. Peter, toward the close of his first epistle, writes to the elders of the churches—"*Shepherd* the flock of God which is among you . . . and when the Chief Shepherd shall appear, ye shall receive a crown of glory that fadeth not away" (1 Pet. 5: 4). He not only shepherds His people, but calls them into a "partnership," a fellowship with Him in the task of shepherding. Peter knew what that meant, for so the Risen Lord had commissioned him, on that memorable morning of the breakfast beside the Lake—"Feed My lambs . . . shepherd My sheep . . . feed My sheep" (John 21: 15–19).

Kings and priests under the old covenant are called shepherds; and Ezekiel rebuked those who "fed" themselves rather than the sheep (Ezek. 34: 2–10). St. Peter warns the "elders" not to behave as "lords over God's heritage" (1 Pet. 5: 3). Whatever authority we exercise over others, whatever position of leadership we might occupy, is delegated; and concerning it we must give an account. This applies not only to the "pastors" (shepherds) of churches, but also Sunday-school teachers, parents, and all who have others committed to their care. For faithfulness and true "shepherding," there is a reward according to the riches of His glory—"a crown of glory that fadeth not away" (1 Pet. 5: 4).

CHAPTER SEVENTEEN

Jehovah-tsidkenu—The LORD our Righteousness

NONE OF the Old Testament names of God anticipates New Testament teaching more clearly than *Jehovah-tsidkenu* does—"the LORD our righteousness" (Jer. 23: 6). This is distinctly a Messianic title. In it, the Gospel truth of justification by faith is enshrined. It declares at once both the demand and the provision of God, made fully known at length in our Lord Jesus Christ.

The righteousness of God is a fundamental revelation of His character. In distinction from the gods of the heathen, who were whatever their devotees wished them to be, *Jehovah* is consistently set forth in the Old Testament as the holy and righteous God, who demands righteousness in His people. His standards are absolute. He who is awful in holiness says, "Be ye holy, for I am holy" (Lev. 11: 44; 19: 2; 20: 7, 26). Nor does He lightly regard defection from that standard—all unrighteousness is sin; and sin banishes from His presence and incurs His wrath. It was so from Eden onwards.

Many Scriptures could be cited to illustrate this: indeed, the whole Bible is an enlargement and demonstration of the fact that God is all-holy, and requires holiness in men, and provides it in Christ. Only foreshadowings of that provision are given in the Old Testament, of course: in the main, the burden of the Law and the prophets is man's estrangement from God through sin, and those means of reconciliation and restoration which anticipated and looked forward to the redeeming grace of Christ our Saviour. From the earliest times, the answer to man's condition and plight was clearly declared to be a *provision of God*: a lamb which typified Him who is "the Lamb of God which taketh away the sin of the world." No attainment of even the best of men could reach the divine standard. Isaiah summed up this discrepancy between man's highest achievements and God's requirements in words which utterly shatter all human complacency—"All our righteousnesses are as filthy rags" (Isa. 64: 6).

How, then, shall a man be justified before God? For equally clearly in Scripture with this unequivocal declaration concerning man's condition, is the fact that God desires his reconciliation and renewal of fellowship with Himself. What man can never achieve or become, however, *God will make him*, by grace through faith. That is the "Gospel" in the Old Testament, as in the New. And this gift of righteousness is not merely a matter of legal standing before God; not merely something that puts him in right relationship with God: it is inwrought into his very character. In theological terminology, it is not only imputed, but imparted.

Now, all this is only partially revealed, in type and foreshadowing, in the Old Testament. Its full declaration had to await the coming of our Lord Jesus Christ, and the proclamation of the Gospel of His grace. It is found in the Old Testament, however; for God is ever consistent: what reaches its full flowering in the New Testament is in embryo in the Old.

In both Testaments this righteousness which God requires is not a mere trait of character or standard of conduct: it is the holiness of God Himself operative in the life which is wholly submissive to Him. It is most intimately related to the Person of God Himself, and is found in men in the measure that their lives are yielded and responsive to the Lord. Isaiah voices this, when he speaks of those that "follow after righteousness . . . that seek the LORD" (Isa. 51: 1). A second essential qualification, also, is indicated in that text—"*follow . . . seek.*" To "hunger and thirst after righteousness" is the only way to progress toward it: but it is a certain way, for the Lord Jesus promised that such should "be filled" (Matt. 5: 6).

The great example, cited by Paul, is Abraham. In his pilgrimage of faith he came into such an intimacy with God that he trusted Him wholly, even to believing in the impossible because God said it. When he had come utterly to an end of all expectation in himself, he "believed God, and it was counted unto him for righteousness" (Rom. 4: 3). So it is with us. When we say, "I know that in me (that is, in my flesh) dwelleth no good thing" (Rom. 7: 18), and look to Him alone, He "reckons" us what we are not! (Rom. 3: 21–26).

What we are not: that would not be a very satisfactory state of affairs, if it were all. It would be but a sham and pretence. And so the truth of imputed righteousness must needs be matched with that of *imparted* righteousness. And *that* is the Gospel. Christ, who died to put away our sins—that we might be forgiven and cleansed from their defilement—rose again for our justification. He not only took our place of condemnation, bearing our sin in our stead, and putting His righteousness to our account: He has come to dwell in His redeemed by His Spirit, to live in us His righteous life. He dwells in us, and we in Him. "If any man be in Christ, he is a new creature: old things are passed away; behold, all things are become new" (2 Cor. 5: 17). "For to me to live is Christ," said Paul; "I live; yet no longer I, but Christ liveth in me" (Phil. 1: 21; Gal. 2: 20). ". . . that the righteousness of the law might be fulfilled in us, who walk not after the flesh, but after the Spirit" (Rom. 8: 4). He who, as *Jehovah-m'qaddishkhem* (the LORD that sanctifieth) *consecrates* us—separates us from sin unto holiness—as *Jehovah-tsidkenu* makes us holy in the practical affairs of everyday life (see pp. 72–74, 146).

Jeremiah saw this "afar off," as he foretold the days when, saith the Lord, "I will raise unto David a righteous Branch, and a King shall reign . . . and this is His name whereby He shall be called, THE LORD OUR RIGHTEOUSNESS" (Jer. 23: 5, 6). This passage is not only Messianic, but millennial. For God's earthly people Israel, this promise still awaits fulfilment: but for the Church, the heirs of the promises, the fulfilment is here and now. We have ample warrant for acclaiming Him *Jehovah-tsidkenu.* He is this to us, in Christ our Lord. Isaiah uttered the same message as Jeremiah, when he linked together the "righteousness" and "salvation" of God (Isa. 51: 5, 8).

St. Paul brings the scriptural revelation on this theme to its culmination in the Epistle to the Romans, where he sets forth in almost terrifying fashion the wrath of God revealed from heaven against all ungodliness and unrighteousness of men, on the one hand; and the manifestation of "the righteousness of God which is by faith of Jesus Christ unto all and upon all them that believe," on the other (1: 18; 3: 22). And so the new covenant counterpart of *Jehovah-tsidkenu* is "Christ our righteousness" (1 Cor. 1: 30). He who knew no sin was "made to be sin for us . . . that we might be made the righteousness of God in Him" (2 Cor. 5: 21).

> Jesus, Thy blood and righteousness
> My beauty are, my glorious dress:
> Midst flaming worlds in these arrayed
> With joy shall I lift up mine head.

Here is the answer—the one only answer—to man's condition and condemnation. Here is his standing before God, and eternal security: for in Christ, His people are presented before the holy God, without spot or wrinkle or any such thing (Eph. 5: 27; Jude 24). Here is the transforming power through which sinners become saints, and ungodly men and women become able to "adorn the doctrine of God our Saviour in all things." God, who demands holiness, provides it in the Person and grace of Christ our Saviour. He is our *Jehovah-tsidkenu*.

CHAPTER EIGHTEEN

Jehovah-shammah—The LORD is There

WITH THIS title, we come to the last of the divine names, in the order of their appearance in the Old Testament. As we said at the start, there is a progressive self-revelation of God in these titles by which He chose to make Himself known, each contributing some new facet of truth regarding His Person and grace. From the fact of His Being, and the power of His works in creation, we have proceeded to see the unfolding of His purposes toward mankind, as the LORD who provides a ransom for sinners; who heals all our (spiritual) diseases; who is our banner in conflict; our sanctifier, who sends peace; is our shepherd; and our righteousness. A fitting culmination is reached in the wondrous promise contained within this last of the Old Testament names of God—*Jehovah-shammah*, "The LORD is there."

This title comes at the very close of the book of Ezekiel (48: 35); and this is its only actual occurrence in Scripture, though —as in the case of other titles—the thought it epitomizes finds frequent expression elsewhere. The prophet tells us that this shall be the name of the city which he saw in vision, and which he describes in detail, with its temple, in chapters 40–48. Ezekiel was, of course, a prophet to the Jews during their exile in Babylon. He called them to repentance, and prophesied their restoration to their own land. Like practically all the prophets, he also foretold events at the end of this age, when the Messiah shall be recognized and received by His people, and shall reign upon the throne of His father David. Joel, prophesying *before* the Captivity, had said: "So shall ye know that I am the LORD your God dwelling in Zion, My holy mountain: then shall Jerusalem be holy . . . for the LORD dwelleth in Zion"

(3: 17, 21). And *after* the exile, Zechariah wrote: "Sing and rejoice, O daughter of Zion: for, lo, I come, and I will dwell in the midst of thee, saith the LORD . . . In that day shall there be upon the bells of the horses, HOLINESS UNTO THE LORD; and upon the pots in the LORD's house . . . yea, every pot in Jerusalem and in Judah shall be holiness unto the LORD of hosts" (2: 10; 14: 20, 21).

Widely varying opinions are held among Evangelical Bible students regarding the interpretation of Ezekiel's visions, and whether or not the temple will be rebuilt in Jerusalem according to his description. It is not our purpose to touch upon this controversy: it is enough that all agree that Ezekiel foretells the *ultimate realization of the purposes of God* for His people, and the *absolute perfection* of their fulfilment.

Under many figures of speech, in both the Old and New Testaments, the final blessedness of the elect, in the presence of God for evermore, is described; and one of the most expressive of these is that of a city. Abraham "looked for a city which hath foundations, whose maker and builder is God" (Heb. 11: 10). Jerusalem, the Holy City, was intended by God to be a "type" and adumbration of that which is to come (Psa. 48: 1-3); but His people lamentably failed to realize and act according to their privileges. Ezekiel once more set before them God's ideal: but its fulfilment awaits the coming down from heaven of the New Jerusalem, which John saw in vision on Patmos (Rev. 21). The glory of that city, like Ezekiel's, lies in this: "The Lord is there" (Rev. 21: 11, 22, 23). That fact is the guarantee that all the promises of God, and all the anticipations of His people, shall be fully and absolutely realized.

This name for God is by no means limited in its application, however, to the city and age to come: it conveys a truth which has been of the greatest reality and comfort to His people in every age. When He delivered the Children of Israel "out of the land of Egypt and the house of bondage," God went before them in a pillar of cloud by day and of fire by night: the visible manifestation of His Presence with them, leading, guiding,

providing, protecting. Whenever any Israelite might fear
regarding their parlous condition—an undisciplined rabble,
in a wilderness—he could look up, by day or night, and assure
his heart: for "the LORD was there." Later, when the tabernacle was built, the Shekinah rested upon and filled the tabernacle, and finally was manifest only in the Holy of Holies—no
longer seen by any save the High Priest; and by him only once
a year. The people who had been able to see the cloud of glory
now had to go forward in faith that God was still with them—
as He was, just as truly as when they could see for themselves
the visible token of His Presence. They had to learn to walk
by faith, not by sight: but it was still true that "the LORD was
there." He was their "very present help" in every kind of
need; and the surety of their inheritance in the land He had
promised them. And so He ever is, to all His people.

When they came into the land, the distinction of Israel from
all the nations of the earth was this: "the LORD was there." So
long as they obeyed and worshipped Him, He was—as
Zechariah said long afterward—"a wall of fire round about,
and the glory in the midst" (2: 5). This was most fully realized
in the "golden age" of the reigns of David and Solomon.
Israel, an insignificant people in a tiny land, were given a glory
and renown supreme in all the world (1 Kings 10: 4-9; 21-29).
But even during Solomon's reign decline set in, and it proceeded with but temporary checks until finally the glory
departed from the temple (Ezek. 10: 4, 18; 11: 23). No longer
was it true that the LORD was there, and very soon the nation
was given into the hands of the Babylonians. Thus Israel
despised their birthright, and forfeited their inestimable privilege. Yet God had not forsaken them: in their very exile He
gave to Ezekiel the vision of a yet more glorious dwelling of
God among His people.

Must we, then, await the fulfilment of apocalyptic vision
before we people of God to-day can enter into the promise,
Jehovah-shammah? In its fullest realization, yes; but there is a
wondrous sense in which this is true in our experience, as it was
in measure in that of the Israelites who "trusted and obeyed."

For the Church is the present temple of God; and every believer is individually a temple wherein His Spirit dwells (1 Cor. 3: 16; 6: 19, 20; Eph. 2: 21, 22). He is with us; and of every regenerate soul it can be said, "The Lord is there."

Now it is one of the most profoundly satisfying aspects of divine revelation that God deals with His elect as *a people* and as *individuals*. We are "members one of another" (Rom. 12: 5; Eph. 4: 25); members of a family (Eph. 3: 15) and of a holy nation (1 Pet. 2: 9). Yet we are saved individually, and are personally the subjects of His care (John 10: 3, 4). We look for a "city"; but we shall never be merely "one in a crowd" (Luke 12: 6–8). No child of His is ever outside His thoughts, or can escape His presence. Wherever one of His people is, "the Lord is *there*."

Hagar proved that. When she thought herself quite alone in the wilderness, the angel of the LORD found her, ". . . and she called the name of the LORD that spake unto her, Thou God seest me" (Gen. 16: 13). It was her way of confessing that the Lord was there.

Jacob, obliged to leave home because of his sharp practice against Esau, lay down in the wilderness, away from home for the first time in his life; and doubtless he felt terribly alone. As he slept, he dreamed of a ladder set up to heaven, with angels of God ascending and descending on it: and God spoke to him, with reassuring words of promise. And Jacob awoke and said, "Surely the LORD is in this place; and I knew it not" (Gen. 28: 16). The Lord was there.

Instances could be multiplied of the Lord's presence with His people in all kinds of places, and amid all circumstances of life —even with those unaware or unheeding of the fact. To mention a few: the sleeping lad, Samuel, in the tabernacle at Shiloh; Elisha's servant in Dothan; Jonah, the self-willed prophet, determined to disobey God's command, in a ship and later in the belly of a great fish; Daniel, in the lions' den, and his companions in the burning fiery furnace; Ezekiel, by the river Kebar. The Psalmist expresses this fact most graphically, under similar imagery to that adopted much later by Francis

Thompson in "The Hound of Heaven." Even if he *wanted* to escape the presence of God, David declared, he could not! "Whither shall I go from Thy Spirit? And whither shall I flee from Thy presence? . . . If I take the wings of the morning, and dwell in the uttermost parts of the sea, even there shall Thy hand lead me, and Thy right hand shall hold me . . ." (Psa. 139: 7–12). In a word, wheresoever a child of God is, "the Lord is there." What comfort, what strength of heart, this assurance bestows!

Blessed and reassuring as this name of God is in its present application, however, we must repeat that its full realization awaits that happy day when the vision of Ezekiel and of St. John shall become glorious reality, and the Lord shall dwell among His people for evermore. The inspired words of prophet and seer set forth the glory and blessedness of that "city" with an eloquence which no other pen can match. Suffice it to say that "we shall see His face" in unclouded vision. With all the redeemed, we shall behold the glory of God in Jesus Christ our Lord. And, no longer in part or by faith; the limitations and besetments of earth forgotten, we shall "be like Him, for we shall see Him as He is" (1 John 3: 2).

"Eye hath not seen, nor ear heard, neither have entered into the heart of man, the things which God hath prepared for them that love Him" (1 Cor. 2: 9). The surety and seal of all the promises; the guarantee of eternal blessedness, is this: "The Lord is there." Fully, finally, without any qualification, *Jehovah-shammah.*

CHAPTER NINETEEN

Abba, Father

MOST PRECIOUS to us of all the titles of God, "Father" is essentially a New Testament name for the One revealed "here a little, there a little" in the various Old Testament titles we have considered: the final unveiling of His Person and grace as "Father" had to await the Incarnation of the Lord Jesus Christ. This simple, yet profound and wondrous name expresses the most intimate relationship with Himself into which He brings the redeemed among men, in Christ. The most satisfying words the human heart can know and tongue utter, "Abba, Father," are the gift of the Gospel to all who believe. It was our Lord Himself who first taught His disciples to say, "Our Father . . ."

Abba is an Aramaic word, meaning "Father." It is very simple to pronounce—*Ab-ba*—so that a baby could say it even before cutting its first tooth. It was indeed the very first word which Hebrew babies of our Lord's day customarily spoke: and undoubtedly was the first word formed by the infant lips of Jesus. The phrase "Abba, Father" is tautological: it repeats the same word in Aramaic and in Greek. The reason for this is that in the original Scriptures the Aramaic *Abba* was translated into the Greek *Pater*, "Father," for the benefit of Greek-speaking readers who could not understand Aramaic. Thus this phrase—which has become a cherished title of God—unites Jew and Gentile believers in a common address to Him as Father. It expresses the fact that the "middle wall of partition" between Jew and Gentile is broken down (Eph. 2:14); we are "all one in Christ Jesus" (Gal. 3:28).

There are anticipations of the title in the Old Testament, in a few scattered texts in which *Jehovah* declares Himself to be a

94

Father to Israel, His chosen people (Exod. 4: 22; Deut. 32: 6; Jer. 31: 9; Hos. 11: 1). But as so used, the word was regarded as metaphorical: a figure of speech, expressing the tender love and patient grace of God toward the nation, unworthy and erring though it was. The Psalmist indicates the response of the true Israelite to this revelation of the heart and will of God, when he says, "Like as a father pitieth his children, so the LORD pitieth them that fear Him" (Psa. 103: 13). It is profoundly illuminating that so Spirit-taught a man as David did not address God as "Father," but said that "*like as a father* . . . so the LORD . . ." In a word, the relationship expressed in the term "Father" was regarded as an analogy only, not an actual fact.

To the devout Jew of Old Testament times, God was so high and awesome, so terrible in majesty, that even His covenant name *Jehovah* was considered too holy to be uttered; to address Him as Father would have seemed intolerable presumption. Later, in the period "between the Testaments," when spiritual life—as distinct from religious punctiliousness and ceremonialism—was at lowest ebb, the term found its way into the liturgy of the Synagogue, and Dr. J. W. Thirtle quotes from it such phrases as "Father of Mercy" and "One is our God: He is our Father: He is our King . . ." But even at this time, when the use of the word became familiar in the worship of the synagogues, it was applied to God only *in relation to the nation*: no individual Jew would have taken it upon his lips in his private prayers and devotions. As Dr. Thirtle adds, "Israel knew that doctrine in its external features, not as to its internal relations."

That knowledge could come only in and through Christ. It is one of the remarkable—though not often noticed—facts concerning our Lord, that His use of the word "Father" in prayer, and regarding His relationship to God, did not give offence, as it would to any true Jew, on any other lips than His. His use of the word was so natural, so self-authenticating, that to the disciples it struck no jarring note of over-familiarity toward God. The Pharisees, of course, realized the implications of it, and charged Him with blasphemy, "making Himself equal with God" (John 5: 18). And indeed, unless He were equal with God His words *were* blasphemous. To address God as "Father" is the right only of the Son, and those to whom He imparts "the Spirit of adoption, whereby we cry, Abba, Father" (Rom. 8: 15; Gal. 4: 6). It was only because Christ could say "My Father" that He could add ". . . and your Father," and proceed to teach us to say, "Our Father . . ." (John 20: 17; Matt. 6: 9). "It is through the revelation of the Son," says Westcott, "that we can find each our personal fellowship with a Father in heaven. And at the same time it is through the revelation of the Son that the idea of Fatherhood is shewn to lie in the very Nature of Godhead itself. In the life and death of Christ there is a revelation unexhausted and inexhaustible of the Father, His Father and our Father." Again Westcott says, with rare felicity of language, "As Son of God Jesus knew the Father perfectly. As Son of man, He revealed the Father perfectly." Here we touch upon the mystery of the Trinity, and would re-affirm as the basis of all our studies the historic faith of the Church expressed in the Athanasian creed: "The Father is God, the Son is God, and the Holy Ghost is God. And yet there are not three Gods, but one God. The Godhead of the Father, and of the Son, and of the Holy Ghost is all one, the Glory equal, the Majesty co-eternal. And in this Trinity none is afore or after the other; none is greater or less than another, but the whole three Persons are co-eternal together and co-equal."

Our Lord Jesus Christ, the eternal Son, came out from the "bosom" of the Father, to reveal Him unto us (John 1: 18). In Him we see and know the Father (John 14: 7–11). Through His redeeming work, He is "bringing many sons unto glory" (Heb. 2: 10). Through faith in Him sinful men, estranged from God, are "born again" (John 3: 3), and in the new birth become "sons of God" (John 1: 12; Rom. 8: 14, 19; Phil. 2: 15; 1 John 3: 1, 2). This sonship is "in Christ"; it is in virtue of relationship to Christ, *the* Son (Gal. 4: 6). The words "Abba, Father" arising in our hearts by the Spirit, are the

witness and seal of our "adoption" (Rom. 8: 15; see p. 180).
They are the most blessed, most wondrous words human lips
can utter. For in knowing God as Father we enter into the
most intimate, privileged, eternal relationship with God, in
Christ. "The name 'Father,'" Westcott truly affirms, "is
indeed the sum of Christian revelation." This one word contains all the values of all the names we have been considering:
it gathers up and sums up them all. "The ideas of power, of
majesty, of leadership, of unutterable awe, which had been
before connected with Deity, are in 'Father' merged in the
idea of tender personal relationship."

We see, then, how erroneous it is to regard the term as
applying to all mankind, and to refer to the Lord's Prayer as
"the universal prayer." There is a sense, of course, in which
God is the "Father of all mankind" as their Creator; but when
our Lord taught His disciples to say "Our Father," He was
most obviously not using the term in that sense. He was indicating a relationship with God into which He was bringing His
disciples by grace through faith. Only the sons of God, through
personal trust in Christ as their Saviour, can, then, truly pray
the Lord's Prayer—which has more fittingly been termed "the
disciples' prayer."

Lest privilege should lead to presumption, however, our
Lord safeguarded this word, by the prefix "Our." *He* addressed
God as "Father," and spoke of Him as "My Father"; but He
taught us to say, "*Our* Father." The relationship we enjoy
with God is one we share with all the elect. It is in fellowship
"with all saints" (Eph. 3: 18) that we say "Our Father"—
and we go on to remind ourselves, as our Lord taught us, that
He is "in heaven," and that hallowed is His Name. For our
Father is God Most High.

While that is so, the tenderness of the relationship and the
wealth of grace expressed in the word "Father" can never be
fully expressed. In our human life we have a faint picture of it
in every cherished tie between father and child, for "like as a
father . . . so God . . ." The word "father" shares with
"mother" the most honoured place in the language of human

relationships; and when applied to God it contains the full value of both words. For all human love finds its source in God, whose nature and name is love. In every beloved bond between parent and child, described in the Word and experienced in everyday life, we have a picture, a dim portrayal, of the Father who "so loved the world that He gave His only begotten Son, that whosoever believeth in Him should not perish, but have everlasting life" (John 3: 16). That love to usward flows out from the mutual love of the Father and the Son. "The Father loveth the Son," said Christ; yet He gave Him for us men and our salvation (John 3: 35; 10: 15, 18; 1 John 4: 10). In the eternal counsels it was so determined: and in fulfilment of that eternal covenant Christ came, and redeemed us unto God. "The Son of God . . . loved me," said St. Paul, "and gave Himself for me" (Gal. 2: 20). That love, "so amazing, so divine," evokes responding love in our dull hearts; and quickens the cry of adoring sonship, "Abba, Father."

> Behold th' amazing gift of love
>   the Father hath bestow'd
> On us, the sinful sons of men,
>   to call us sons of God!
>
> Concealed as yet this honour lies,
>   by this dark world unknown,
> A world that knew not when He came,
>   ev'n God's eternal Son.
>
> High is the rank we now possess;
>   but higher we shall rise;
> Though what we shall hereafter be
>   is hid from mortal eyes:
>
> Our souls, we know, when He appears,
>   shall bear His image bright;
> For all His glory, full disclos'd,
>   shall open to our sight.
>
> A hope so great, and so divine,
>   may trials well endure;
> And purge the soul from sense and sin,
>   as Christ Himself is pure.

PART II

NAMES AND TITLES OF OUR
LORD JESUS CHRIST

There is none other name under heaven given among men, whereby we must be saved—Acts 4: 12.

"The Eternal Speaking Word, which created all things, did in the fullness of time move itself in the name Jesus, according to its highest and deepest humility."—JACOB BOHEME.

"It may seem remarkable that the beautiful titles of Jehovah found in the Old Testament are not in the New: but a little deeper consideration will show the reason for this. Under the Old Testament dispensation, it was necessary to teach even the redeemed people of God by many different pictures and types, because though delivered from bondage, their deliverance was physical, and in heart they were still separated from God through sin, and by nature knew nothing of spiritual access and worship. 'The only-begotten of the Father' had not yet been 'manifested in the flesh,' and they could not therefore 'know the LORD' (Jer. 31: 34), except by figures and types. Our light is, of course, infinitely greater than theirs; for in the New Testament we find 'Jehovah' revealing Himself in the *Person* of His beloved Son: and we have but to look upon the LORD Jesus Christ as 'Jehovah,' and endeavour to realize Him in all His beauties and perfection, to see that every one of the Old Testament titles is to be found embodied in Him."—H. W. WEBB-PEPLOE.

CHAPTER TWENTY

Old Testament Prophetic Names of Christ

O N THE road to Emmaus the risen Lord drew near to
two disconsolate disciples and, "beginning at Moses
and all the prophets, He expounded unto them in all
the Scriptures the things concerning Himself" (Luke 24: 27).
This is our warrant for seeing Christ "in all the Scriptures."
His Incarnation and atoning work are not only declared in
prophetic utterances, but are shown forth in types, metaphors,
and analogies. Some of these we shall touch upon, in considering such titles as King, Priest, and the Lamb of God; others are
outside the scope of this book—e.g., the various "types" of
tabernacle and temple which prefigure His Person or atoning
ministry. He is the "Wisdom" personified in Proverbs: yet
this is not strictly a prophetic title (but see "Counsellor,"
below). Several phrases in the Song of Solomon, which have
become a treasured part of the language of devotion of Christian
people, such as "Chiefest among ten thousand," "Rose of
Sharon," and "Lily of the Valley," are yet not strictly titles of
Christ—although they may rightly be regarded as extolling
Him, and worthily be applied to Him. Passing over all these,
however, we have a number of indisputable titles of our Lord,
given by prophetic inspiration, which should have fully prepared His people to recognize and welcome Him when He
came, and which are the rich heritage of the Church from the
Old Testament Scriptures.

Before we consider these, however, we must touch upon
His pre-Incarnation appearances to men, as the "Angel of
Jehovah," and in other theophanies (Gen. 18: 1–33; 31: 11–13;
32: 24–30; Exod. 14: 19; Judges 6: 11, etc.). In the dawn-
ings of human history; in the experiences of the patriarchs;

and in the early days of Israel's nationhood, God appeared in human form on certain occasions: and there can be no doubt that, in every case, it was the Second Person of the Trinity, "the visible Image of the invisible God," whom men beheld and whose voice they heard (cf. Isa. 6: 1–5; John 12: 41).

The name "Jesus," given to Him by divine command at His birth, declares His Deity: all the Old Testament names of God, therefore, belong to Him and find their fulfilment in Him. The Messianic utterances of psalmists and prophets are consonant with, and complementary to, the revelation given in the names we have already considered.

> His name encircles every grace
> That God as man could show. . . .

The earliest anticipation in Scripture of the coming of Christ is contained in the words of the Lord to the serpent after the Fall, "I will put enmity between thee and the woman, and between thy seed and her seed: and it shall bruise thy head, and thou shalt bruise his heel" (Gen. 3: 15). This can only be understood as referring to Christ, however, in the light of subsequent Scriptures. A somewhat clearer intimation was given to Abram, in the promise, "In thee shall all the families of the earth be blessed," and the expansion of that promise in the experience of the patriarch until—as our Lord stated— "Abraham saw My day; he saw it, and was glad" (John 8: 56). The earliest explicit Messianic prediction, however, is in Jacob's dying words concerning Judah—"The sceptre shall not depart from Judah . . . until Shiloh come" (Gen. 49: 10). Here we have the first of the prophetic titles of Christ:

(i) SHILOH. A good deal of scholarly discussion has taken place concerning this word and its context; but, as H. L. Ellison says, "the majority opinion among scholars seems to have veered round to what is almost certainly the oldest interpretation of *shiloh*, viz. *shel-lo*, i.e. 'he whose right it is '" (see Ezek. 21: 27). Some expositors affirm that the word means "Peacemaker," and link it with the Messianic title given later by Isaiah, "Prince of Peace" (see below): but Hebrew scholars

do not support this view. However that may be, this prophecy
of Jacob is the earliest intimation of the Kingship of our Lord
Jesus Christ. It foretold that He would be of the royal tribe of
Judah; but that He would not wield a temporal sceptre—
indeed, power hitherto vested in the tribe would pass from
Judah at His coming: yet He would exercise a sovereignty of a
different character, by eternal right. All this was literally fulfilled when Joseph, the heir of the house of David, went in
obedience to the decree of a foreign ruler, with Mary his
espoused wife, from their home in Nazareth to Bethlehem—
where Jesus was born, the Messiah, the Shiloh foretold so long
before, by the patriarch. If only the Jews throughout their
history had heeded this first of prophecies concerning the
Christ, how many mistakes they would have avoided!

Further pre-eminent aspects of the Person and ministry of
the Messiah were later indicated by Moses, in his promise to
the people that "the LORD God will raise up unto thee a
Prophet . . . like unto me" (Deut. 18: 15–19). Both Peter and
Stephen affirmed that this prediction was fulfilled in Christ
(Acts 3: 22; 7: 37). Moses was the "prophet *par excellence*
(Deut. 34: 10), the perfect spokesman and revealer of God"
(H. L. Ellison); and he also performed priestly tasks (Exod.
24: 3–8). He therefore prefigures Christ as both—

(ii) PROPHET and PRIEST—and all the ordinances and pro-
visions of the Law are a "commentary" upon this two-fold
office of our Lord (see pp. 114, 134).

In the Messianic psalms are clear predictions of Christ as
the Son of God (2: 2); the Holy One (16: 10); the Redeemer
(22: 1–18); and King (2: 6; 24: 7–10). A full-length "portrait"
of Him was therefore given thus early in Israel's history. All
that had been thus foreshadowed in the writings of Moses and
the ceremonies of the Law, and uttered in the inspired songs of
psalmists, found fuller and clearer expression, however, in the
Messianic pronouncements of the prophets. Isaiah is, of course,
outstandingly the fore-teller of Christ; and his first designation
of Him is—

(iii) THE BRANCH (*tsemach*)—literally, a shoot or sprout,

springing from the root of a cut-down tree (Isa. 4: 2). Here, He is called "the Branch of *Jehovah*"—that is, one come in fulfilment of the divine purposes and pledges, at a time when such fulfilment would seem not only unlikely but practically impossible. He would be, not merely raised up by God, but *Jehovah* Himself. It is doubtful if even Isaiah realized the full wonder and implication of the prophecy he was given by the Spirit to utter. For his words embraced more than the first coming of Christ: they anticipated that time when "the fruit of the earth shall be excellent and comely for them that are escaped of Israel." The context is one of judgment, and the promise shines as a ray of light amid darkness. Israel shall be chastened sore for her sins: only a remnant shall escape; but for that remnant the prospect is glorious. The promises of God to Israel are ultimately to be realized, after long subjugation and suffering through their sin. Seemingly "cut down to the ground," they shall acknowledge and acclaim the Lord Jesus Christ as their Messiah and King.

The term "Branch," however, has also specific reference to the divine promises to David, for "there shall come forth a rod out of the stem of Jesse, and a Branch shall grow out of his roots" (Isa. 11: 1). The Hebrew word for "rod" is *choter*, and for "Branch" (in this text), *netzer*: but both of these mean practically the same as *tsemach*, a sprout or shoot. In 11: 1, the Messiah is identified as both "the root and offspring of David" (v. 10; Rev. 22: 16); born "of David's royal line," yet, as the Creator, the "Root" from which David sprang. Here is the clearest intimation of the Incarnation: that the Messiah would be both the Eternal and the Son of man. But He would "sprout" from the cut-down stem of Jesse—a remarkable prediction that, despite all the national aspirations centring in the Davidic line, the family would be neglected and reduced—as was literally fulfilled when Jesus was born in a stable and reared in the home of a village carpenter. Albeit He was a King: but the characteristic of His reign would be, not earthly pomp and power, but righteousness (Jer. 23: 5, 6). He would "execute judgment and righteousness in the land" (Jer. 33: 15).

The vision of His reign, so different from that of the kings of the earth, becomes ever clearer; and Zechariah culminates the prophetic fore-glimpses of His glory—not only as King but also Priest—in glowing words: "Behold the man whose name is The BRANCH; and He shall . . . bear the glory, and shall sit and rule upon the throne; and He shall be a priest upon His throne . . ." (Zech. 6: 12, cf. 3: 8). Prof. F. F. Bruce observes that "the probable meaning of Zechariah 6: 13 is, 'there shall be a priest beside his throne'; this explains the following clause, 'and the counsel of peace shall be between them both.' In the 'type,' prince (Zerubbabel) and priest (Joshua) are separate: in the Antitype they are One."

This one title alone, however, should have left no devout reader of the Hebrew Scriptures in any doubt regarding the manner of Messiah's coming and the nature of His reign: but it is only part of the prophetic portrait. Isaiah also foretold that He should be—

(iv) IMMANUEL—"God with us" (Isa. 7: 14). Controversy has encompassed the prediction of His being born of a virgin, but it cannot rob us of the inexpressible wonder and grace of the coming into our human life of God Himself, through the miracle of Virgin Birth.

It is not within the scope of this book to discuss the various theories put forward by scholars regarding this prophecy: those who desire it will find a thoroughly satisfying examination of the several differing interpretations, from an Evangelical viewpoint, in Dr. Edward J. Young's *Studies in Isaiah*. We confine ourselves to a Biblical study of the divine names and titles, and unreservedly accept Matthew's statement that this prophecy concerning Immanuel referred to the coming of Christ (Matt. 1: 23). Undoubtedly there was an immediate fulfilment of the "sign" to unbelieving Ahaz; but the prophetic word went far beyond that, to the Messiah. Many children in Israel were named Immanuel, in expression of faith that God was with His people—just as many were called Jesus, "Jehovah is the Saviour": but none truly bare these names until He came who is the fulfilment and true expression of them—God with us; Jehovah the Saviour. Whether the Jews realized it or not, in this name Immanuel, as used by Isaiah, was a further clear intimation of the Incarnation. In Jesus, God came down to live among, and to redeem sinful men; now exalted, He is with us still by His Spirit.

From this prediction, Isaiah passes swiftly to that remarkable constellation of titles which follows the promise of a "Child" to be born—indicating His true Humanity, and "Son" to be given—His true Deity: "God's gratuitous gift on which man had no claim" (Isa. 9: 6, 7). His name should be called—

(v) WONDERFUL COUNSELLOR. It is generally agreed that these two words form one title, in keeping with the three double-word names which follow. Some expositors cling to the rendering of the Authorized Version, however; and it certainly has more than mere sentiment and tradition to commend it— more even than Handel's magnificent musical setting in the *Messiah*! WONDERFUL is in itself a deeply suggestive name. It is the word rendered "secret" in the reply of the Angel of Jehovah to Manoah, who had asked His name (Judges 13: 18): "it both expresses and hides the Incomprehensible" (F. C. Jennings). He is wonderful, says Fausset, not only in what He says and does, but in the unfathomable mysteries of His Person. "If we contemplate His works, both in creation and redemption," observes Andrew Searle, "we shall find some legible characters of this WONDERFUL LORD indelibly written upon them all. All that Christ did, and all that He suffered, both to introduce an everlasting righteousness and to expiate sin, was wonderful and glorious." Not only so: He is the COUNSELLOR of His people. Himself needing none (Rom. 11: 33, 34), for He is the Fount of all wisdom and knowledge (Prov. 8: 14), He imparts of His counsel to those who seek it (Psa. 16: 7; 25: 9; Isa. 25: 1; 28: 29). The admonition and illumination and leading of the Lord has none of the limitations inevitably characterizing all human counsel: for He is omniscient, the only wise God, the Wonderful Counsellor.

That is but the first of this quartette of designations. He is also—

(vi) THE MIGHTY GOD (*El Gibbor*). He who voluntarily assumed the frailties of true manhood, sin apart, was yet Very God: here is explicit refutation of *kenotic* theories and all other views which would deprive Him of Deity (see p. 30). This was He who was "brought as a lamb to the slaughter." This was He who was "wounded for our transgressions; bruised for our iniquities." This was He whom they taunted upon the tree! The Mighty God! As if to emphasize this truth—admittedly impossible to grasp apart from the enlightenment and enabling of the Spirit—the prophet adds title to title: the Messiah would be also—

(vii) THE EVERLASTING FATHER, literally "Father of Eternity." This is a most emphatic assertion of His Deity. We, in the light of the New Testament revelation of the Trinity, are careful not to "confuse the Persons" of the Godhead, by using the name of One for Another; but Isaiah was speaking, by inspiration, long before men had apprehended the truth of the Triune Nature of God, and he uses a term not only expressive of the Eternal Being of the One who should come, but also conveying the thought that He would be the Giver of eternal life. Moreover, He is—

(viii) THE PRINCE OF PEACE. The "Pole-star" of this constellation of titles, "Prince of Peace" speaks to the deepest needs of the human heart: it is of utmost comfort and reassurance to every believer individually, and to the people of God as a community. In the first instance, it contained a particularly desirable promise to Israel. The nation was constantly harassed by war, their little land being the "cockpit" in which the surrounding great powers often waged their battles. Peace was the one supreme longing of the true Israelite. It was promised in the reign of the Messiah. How appropriate also, in that respect, is this title of Christ to our own war-ridden generation! Through the reign of the Prince of Peace alone will real peace come to this troubled earth, not only for Israel, but all the nations. But that is not the deepest note of the title. Hearts distressed through conviction concerning sin have ever realized that "there is no peace . . . to the wicked." Peace with

God, and consequently peace within, are possible through Christ alone. He *made* peace through the blood of His Cross. He *is* our peace (Rom. 5: 1; Eph. 2: 14; Col. 1: 20); *Jehovah-shalom* (see p. 75). To every trustful heart, He is the Prince of Peace: God our Saviour!

In all these titles the glory and greatness of the Messiah are proclaimed, and Jews reading them would be justified in thinking of earthly supremacy and splendour—withal that some contain hints of the *Via Dolorosa*. These predictions are matched by others, however, which present so different a picture that we can understand the error of the Jews in regarding them as applying to some other person from the Messiah. For Isaiah also spoke of a—

(ix) SERVANT of Jehovah (Isa. 42: 1), who would accomplish His purposes through suffering (52: 13–53: 12). He was the ELECT in the eternal counsels of the Godhead, unto this redeeming work (Isa. 42: 1).

As in the case of the "Immanuel" prophecy of Isaiah (7: 14; see p. 105), the Messianic application of these "suffering Servant" passages is strongly disputed by the critics. It is not our purpose to become involved in the complex arguments put forward in support of differing suggestions—that "Suffering Servant" was a collective term for the nation; or a device of the prophet for referring to himself; or that this imagery was adopted from a pagan myth of a dying and rising god, etc. Again we would refer the reader, for a thorough discussion of these matters, to Dr. Edward J. Young's *Studies in Isaiah*. We confine ourselves to a Biblical study of the divine titles, and accept the "Suffering Servant" passages as referring prophetically to the earthly life and ministry and atoning death of our Lord Jesus Christ. It needed the actual coming of Christ, and the subsequent revelation by the Spirit, to unveil the full mystery. The Messiah would come, Isaiah foretold, not in blinding splendour, but in great humility; without ceasing to be the Eternal Son, co-equal with the Father, He would yet be made in the form of a servant: and being found in fashion as a man would humble Himself, becoming obedient

unto death, even the death of the Cross (Phil. 2: 6–8). Only
so could He fulfil the eternal counsels; only so could He reign
in righteousness, without condemning to eternal doom sinful
men—which includes all mankind, for all have sinned and
come short of the glory of God. Only through death could
He redeem sinners: and only through redemption could He
establish His Kingdom. These seemingly contradictory prophecies are therefore not incompatible; they are mutually
dependent—each can be realized only because the others
are true. He shall reign, because He redeemed. He redeemed, because He is THE GLORIOUS LORD (Isa. 33: 21; see p.
147). He who came in weakness and submission is coming again
in power and great glory.

Thus these titles present the Saviour who is King: the King
who is Saviour. The glory of His Person is enhanced by the
glory of His grace. The King-Priest is, finally, the—

(x) LEADER AND COMMANDER OF HIS people (Isa. 55: 4): the
Captain of our salvation—see p. 142 (Heb. 2: 10). For His
coming we wait! In the A.V. is a graphic phrase, often
regarded as a title of Christ—"the desire of all nations"
(Haggai 2: 7); but as H. L. Ellison says rightly, "The A.V.
rendering is based on the Vulgate, and is incompatible with the
Hebrew. We must either render as in the R.V., 'the desirable
things of all nations shall come,' or perhaps better, 'the desired
of all nations shall come,' i.e., all the nations which Jehovah
desires and chooses." He adds very truly, "Obviously for his
hearers this implied the coming as Messiah as well"; but the
phrase in question can hardly be regarded as a title of Christ.
Nevertheless, the underlying truth proclaimed in the passage
is the expectation and "blessed hope" of all who "love His
appearing." Thus the glory of His Second Advent was anticipated in Old Testament prophecy, even as His humiliation at
Bethlehem and Golgotha was clearly foretold. His coming
will be the consummation of the ages, and the "fullness of joy"
for all who love Him.

CHAPTER TWENTY-ONE

Jesus

O F ALL the names ascribed to our Lord Jesus Christ, the best loved by Christian people of every race and generation, is the simplest—the human name, JESUS. This was the name which His mother whispered lovingly, as He lay in her arms a helpless babe; the name by which He was known to all in Nazareth of Galilee, as He grew through boyhood to manhood. Not that Mary chose the name for Him; it had been given Him before His birth, by the angel Gabriel, in his announcement to Mary herself (Luke 1: 31), and to Joseph, that the child to be born of his betrothed was the Son of God—"Thou shalt call His name JESUS: for He shall save His people from their sins" (Matt. 1: 21). It is the name appointed by God the Father, not only for the brief time of our Lord's sojourn upon earth, but as the name by which He shall be worshipped for evermore (Phil. 2: 10, 11). It enshrines and expresses the mystery of His Person, and the wonder of His redeeming grace.

> Jesus, name of matchless splendour!
> Name all other names above
> Glorious Son of God incarnate,
> King of Kings, and Lord of love!

This is the name used most frequently in the Gospels. It was His personal name, and the one by which the evangelists almost invariably refer to Him. Yet, most arrestingly, there is no record of anyone addressing Him by it—not even His own disciples—with the possible exception of the dying thief (Luke 23: 42, R.V.). Despite the intimacy of fellowship which the twelve enjoyed with Him, they never adopted toward Him the familiarity that was natural among themselves, but addressed Him with titles of respect, such as "Lord" or "Master." To the people of Nazareth, among whom He had been brought up, He was known, naturally enough, as "Jesus, the son of Joseph"—which was also His legal status (John 1: 45; 6: 42); and in Mark 6: 3, "son of Mary": but the latter expression had, of course, none of the implication added to it by the Roman Catholic Church. Among the people generally, He was sometimes called "Jesus of Nazareth" or "Jesus the prophet of Nazareth of Galilee," and occasionally "Jesus the Nazarene," "Jesus the Son of David," and other Messianic titles.

Jesus was a common name among the Jews of those days. It is the Greek rendering of the Hebrew Joshua—which itself is a contraction of Jehoshua, "Jehovah is Salvation." Its origin is interesting. The son of Nun, Moses' servant, was named Hoshea, or Oshea, which means "Salvation," but Moses re-named him Jehoshua (Num. 13: 16), probably in anticipation of the great task to which God had appointed him, and as a testimony that the "salvation" or deliverance to be wrought through him would be given by Jehovah. As borne by Joshua, this name was an expression of faith in God, and testimony to God; in Jesus, the true, deep significance of the name was fulfilled. God had visited His people, in the Person of His Son, to save them. The name of Jesus declares His redeeming intent toward sinful men: it contains within it the very essence of the Gospel.

A most interesting fact is pointed out by Dr. Wilbur M. Smith concerning the verb *yasha*, "to save," from which comes the word "Joshua." The first occurrence of this verb, in Exodus 14: 30, embraces all that the word was later to mean in the Scriptures. Dr. Smith observes, "This testifies to that great truth, that the first occurrence of any major word in divine revelation is the acorn out of which all that pertains to it was ultimately to grow."

As time went on and our Lord's Messianic office was realized, the title "Christ" was added to "Jesus," and eventually the full designation "Lord Jesus Christ" came into most frequent use. "Jesus" gradually took on a new significance: what had been an ordinary name, borne by many, became distinctive and apart. Here we observe for the first time an important fact which—as Professor B. B. Warfield demonstrates so convincingly in his book, *The Lord of Glory*—obtains with all the names of our Lord: that He imparted to them a richer and deeper value than they had ever before possessed. What He was and did invested the names He bore with a new content of meaning. So with "Jesus": its significance grows as the Gospel story proceeds. As time went on the Jews refrained from using it for their sons, because of its association with the Crucified; and Christians naturally forebore to do so. It became a name unique—His alone. Yet the paradox remains that, although reverence for Him forbade the familiar use of the name "Jesus," that name became increasingly precious to His people. It evokes the deepest response of faith and love, and stirs to utmost devotion. For Jesus is the name of God who became Man; it declares His true Humanity; it expresses all that was contained within the Old Testament "Immanuel" (see p. 105).

In Jesus, God has come down to meet our need. In Him we find the answer to the age-old longing, "Show me Thy glory." God, who at sundry times and in divers manners spake in time past unto the fathers by the prophets, hath . . . spoken unto us in His Son. The unclouded revelation of God is given us in Jesus: the fullness of the divine grace is bestowed upon us in Him.

The comfort of the stupendous truths expressed so simply in the one word, Jesus, is therefore immeasurable. The Old Testament had assured His people that God "knoweth our frame: He remembereth that we are dust" (Psa. 103: 14); but Jesus, moving among the multitudes and having compassion on the sick and lonely and needy—that brings home to us far more wondrously the grace and goodness and providential care of God. That God the Son became Man to bear our sins in His own body upon the tree, assures us of a love that "passeth knowledge," and makes John 3: 16 the sweetest text in the Bible.

Jesus, having lived among men, Himself truly Man albeit Very God, returned to the throne on high, in our human likeness, now glorified. In the glory, for ever "the Man Christ Jesus," our Advocate and High Priest, He bears still the human name, "that at the name of Jesus every knee should bow."

> Where high the heavenly temple stands,
> The house of God not made with hands,
> A great high priest our nature wears,
> The guardian of mankind appears.

No wonder His people cherish the name of Jesus! It bears witness that our God is our Saviour; that the occupant of the throne of heaven is the One who went about doing good. It inspires us to come with boldness unto the throne of grace, knowing assuredly that we shall find grace to help in time of need.

Hymnists and mystics have alike rejoiced in extolling the name of Jesus; missionaries and preachers count it their greatest privilege to declare the grace and the glory of that matchless name; and the humblest believer trusts it through life and in the hour of death.

> Jesus, the name high over all,
>   In earth, or hell, or sky;
> Angels and men before it fall,
>   And devils fear and fly.

> Jesus, the name to sinners dear,
>   The name to sinners given;
> It scatters all their guilty fear,
>   It turns their hell to heaven.

Messiah

CHAPTER TWENTY-TWO

Christ

As "JESUS" is the personal name of our Lord, so "Christ" is His official title. It is the Greek equivalent of the Hebrew "Messiah," or "Anointed"—a term which gathered up all the Jewish expectation of the "coming one" foreshadowed in many Old Testament Scriptures, yet concerning whom opinion was so vague even among the rabbis and students of the Holy Oracles. Perhaps the clearest conception of Him was as "great David's greater son"—a descendant of David who should come to the throne of Israel, endued with wisdom and might by Jehovah, to make Israel the most powerful and prosperous nation on earth. But that obviously did not exhaust the meaning of the term, for not only were kings anointed, but also priests and occasionally prophets (1 Kings 19: 16), in symbolism of the divine grace upon them, for the discharge of their office. So the Messiah would be also a spiritual leader: prophet, priest, and king (see page 103); and unto all three offices our Lord could say, "The Spirit of *Jehovah* is upon Me, because He hath anointed Me . . ." (Luke 4: 18). And Peter afterward declared, "God anointed Jesus of Nazareth with the Holy Ghost . . ." (Acts 10: 38). By the time He came, however, the earthly expectations practically obscured the spiritual: the nation longed only for a powerful ruler who would free them from the dominion of Rome and raise Israel to supremacy among the nations of the earth. That false conception did not invalidate the true mission of the Messiah; but it did render them incapable of recognizing Him when He appeared among them.

Jesus is declared to be the Christ in Matthew's genealogy (Matt. 1: 16); and He was so heralded by the angel who announced His advent to the shepherds (Luke 2: 11). At His presentation in the temple, Simeon uttered his *Nunc Dimittis*, testifying that this Babe was "the Lord's Christ" (Luke 2: 26). Magi came from the East, asking, "Where is He that is born King of the Jews?" Hearing this, Herod gathered all the chief priests and scribes together, and "demanded of them where *the Christ* should be born" (Matt. 2: 4). Thus was He attested by heaven, and recognized by Jew and Gentile; king and priests and people. The failure of the many to receive Him was therefore all the more culpable.

Thirty years later John the Baptist plainly declared, in answer to questions regarding his identity, "I am not the Christ" (John 1: 20); and he pointed to Jesus as the One he had been commissioned to announce—clearly indicating that He was the Christ. As such, several of John's disciples attached themselves to Jesus (vv. 41, 45).

The title "Christ" was never used by our Lord concerning Himself, however; probably because of the debased conceptions the people had come to attach to it. But when the woman of Samaria said, "I know that Messias cometh, which is called Christ," He replied, "I that speak unto thee am He" (John 4: 25, 26). And when Peter made his great confession at Caesarea Philippi, "Thou art the Christ, the Son of the living God," He exclaimed, "Blessed art thou, Simon Bar-jona: for flesh and blood hath not revealed it unto thee, but My Father which is in heaven" (Matt. 16: 16, 17). Moreover, He made regular use of other titles of Messianic significance—especially "Son of Man"—which were in fact claims to be the Christ.

Apart from these references, the use of the title is infrequent in the Gospels. But it becomes prominent again—significantly enough—in the record of His trial before the Sanhedrin. When the false witnesses against Him had contradicted one another, Caiaphas put Him on oath and said, "I adjure Thee by the living God, that Thou tell us whether Thou be the Christ, the Son of God" (Matt. 26: 63). That was the ground upon which the leaders and representatives of the nation condemned Him. For His claim to be the Christ, He was crucified.

At Pentecost, the key-note of Peter's sermon was the emphatic declaration, "God hath made that same Jesus, whom ye have crucified, both Lord and Christ" (Acts 2: 36). That theme was taken up by Paul, who, in the synagogues of the various cities he visited during his missionary journeys, reasoned with the Jews out of the Scriptures, "opening and alleging that Christ must needs have suffered, and risen again from the dead; and that this Jesus, whom I preach unto you, is Christ" (Acts 17: 3; cf. 26: 23).

The name had no such significance, however, for the Gentiles to whom Paul preached the Gospel; yet we find the apostle using it in all his epistles to the Gentile Churches. Here we witness a development in its significance—the title taking on a new meaning, in its relation to Him. No longer is it a mere title, the Messiah, the Anointed; it has become a personal name, yet with all the value of "Messiah" included within it. In a word, "the Christ" has become "Christ." Sometimes it stands alone; at other times it is joined to "Jesus"—Jesus Christ. And as the New Testament proceeds, and the realization of His Person and glory is more clearly apprehended, the prefix "Lord" is attached; and finally, the full designation by which all true Christians delight supremely to address Him, "our Lord Jesus Christ."

As such, His people recognize Him to be indeed the One in whom all the Old Testament prophecies concerning the Messiah are fulfilled, even more abundantly than prophets, psalmists and seers could conceive. He is our "Prophet, Priest, and King." He is "great David's greater Son" (Rom. 1: 3; Rev. 5: 5); the Prophet of whom Moses spoke (Deut. 18: 15, 18); and our great High Priest (Heb. 4: 14; 8: 1; 9: 11; 10: 21). As the name "Jesus" bespeaks His true Humanity, so "Christ" declares His Deity: He is God the Son, the Second Person of the Blessed Trinity. The name Christ, said Warfield, "is weighted with the entire content of His claims." It is the divine counterpart of "Jesus." As His human name assures us that our God is our Saviour, so His divine name declares that our Saviour is our God.

CHAPTER TWENTY-THREE

Lord

W E HAVE already seen that the name "Jesus" and the title "Christ," familiar as they were at the time of our Saviour's earthly life, took on a new meaning when actually borne by Him: and this was so with all His names and titles. Of none was this more marked than in the case of "Lord." At first it was a mere respectful manner of address, equivalent to "Sir," but before the New Testament closes the title has come to possess all the weight of Deity.

The Greek word *kurios* had a wide range of application. It is used in the New Testament for the "owner," "lord" or "master" of slaves or property; and as a term of respect toward a superior. In the Septuagint, the Greek Version of the Old Testament, the divine titles *Adonai* and *Jehovah* are rendered "Lord" (*Kurios*). As applied to Jesus it was usually just a respectful courtesy, except on the part of His disciples, to whom He was truly "Master." But even in their case the term had at first no clear connotation. It expressed their faith in Him, and trustful submission; but in a vague manner, as they had not really thought out their relationship to Him. From this nebulous beginning we can trace through the New Testament the growing awareness of the true significance of this most apposite title, "Lord."

Like "Jesus" and "Christ," this designation had been given Him at His birth, in the announcement of the angel who proclaimed to the shepherds, "Unto you is born . . . Christ the Lord" (Luke 2: 11); and at the beginning of His public ministry John the Baptist called the nation to "Prepare ye the way of the Lord" (Luke 3: 4). In both these references it plainly means *Jehovah*. But Israel did not heed: He had come unto His own, and they received Him not. The disciples believed in Him and had given their lives to His service: but some time elapsed before even Peter, for example, had an experience which led him to exclaim, "Depart from me; for I am a sinful man, O Lord" (Luke 5: 8). That marked a distinctive stage in his realization of the Person of his Master.

As time went on, Jesus Himself used the word with clearer implication. While He made no attempt to define the term, He gave it a ring of absolute authority in such statements as "the Son of Man is Lord of the Sabbath" (Mark 2: 28). It was not until the last week of His ministry, however, that He made use of the title in a way which left His claim to divine authority unmistakable. On Palm Sunday He sent for the ass and her foal, with the words, "The Lord hath need of them" (Matt. 21: 3). In disputation with the Pharisees He tacitly declared Himself to be David's Lord (Matt. 22: 41-46). On the Mount of Olives, when instructing His disciples concerning impending events and His Second Coming, He repeatedly exhorted them to "Watch . . . for ye know not what hour your Lord doth come" (Matt. 24: 42; cf. v. 46; 25: 13, etc). In the Upper Room He said, "Ye call me Master and Lord: and ye say well; for so I am" (John 13: 13).

With all this, their understanding was still limited, until after the resurrection: then the new discovery of them all, concerning the Person of their Lord, was expressed by Thomas in his unreserved confession, "My Lord and my God" (John 20: 28). From that time onwards "Lord," as applied to Him, is a divine title: the entire confession of Thomas is encompassed within it. It truly contains all the significance of *Jehovah*.

In the Book of Acts, "Lord" is the most frequently used title: it replaces "Jesus" as the "narrative name." Use of the personal name "Jesus" would doubtless now be considered too great a familiarity; and "Christ" was too formal. So "the Lord" took on the quality of a name rather than a title: but one tinged with the respect which was recognized to be His due. It had the advantage, too, of conveying the thought of *relationship*: He was not only Jesus, the Man in the midst of the throne; and not only Christ, who had come out from the bosom of the Father to redeem sinful men, and returned as their representative on high; but also the *Lord* of all who trusted and loved Him, and had found in Him salvation and eternal life. To call Him "Lord" was both a confession of faith and loyalty, and a claim to be His disciple.

In the Epistles, a fuller unveiling of the glory of the exalted Lord Jesus is given in the various usages of this title. He is shown to be the Lord, not only of the redeemed, but also of all created beings (Rom. 14: 9; Heb. 1: 3–6). He is indeed, as Peter declared to Cornelius, "Lord of all" (Acts 10: 36). He is the King of kings and Lord of lords (1 Tim. 6: 15). He is the Lord of glory (1 Cor. 2: 8). To Him is given the "name above every name . . . that every tongue should confess that Jesus Christ is Lord, to the glory of God the Father" (Phil. 2: 11). Harking back as it does to Isaiah 45: 23, this verse practically makes the assertion that "Jesus Christ is *Jehovah*"; cf. 1 Peter 3: 15, "sanctify in your hearts Christ as Lord," R.V., in the light of the Old Testament passage to which it alludes, Isaiah 8: 13, "*Jehovah* of hosts, Him shall ye sanctify . . ."

How blessed are they, then, who in loving trust can call Him "Lord." The uttering of the one word in sincerity is a seal of salvation, for "no man can say that Jesus is Lord, but by the Holy Ghost" (1 Cor. 12: 3). The word expresses the whole majesty of His Person, and the wonder of His redeeming grace in bringing His sinful creatures into a relationship with Him of trust and love. The Lord of glory is *our* Lord and our God.

CHAPTER TWENTY-FOUR

Son of Man

A SPECIAL significance attaches to the title "Son of man," because this was the designation which our Lord habitually used concerning Himself. It is not found in the New Testament on any other lips than His own—except when His questioners quoted His words (John 12: 34), and in the one instance of Stephen's ecstatic exclamation in the moment of his martyrdom, "Behold, I see the heavens opened, and the Son of man standing on the right hand of God" (Acts 7: 56). It is clearly a Messianic title, as the Jews recognized (John 12: 34). That being so, why did He not use the more explicit titles, "Christ" or "Son of David"? The reason probably lies in the nationalistic associations of those names: they had come to represent the earthly aspirations of the Jews. Our Lord's ministry and message did not conform to those expectations: so He chose to call Himself "Son of man" in order to direct their attention to a different line of prophetic teaching from that which they had so grievously misunderstood.

Most Bible students are agreed that our Lord took the phrase "Son of man" from Daniel 7: 13, and intended its use to direct attention to that Scripture. There, then, we shall find a key to its meaning, as used by Him. In that chapter, the prophet is given a vision of the successive world empires, under the imagery of beasts—the lion (Babylonian), bear (Medo-Persian), leopard (Grecian), and the fourth indescribable beast, "dreadful and terrible" (Roman). After this followed the ten horns, and the "little horn" rising up among them—typifying the disintegration of the Roman Empire, and subsequent struggle for power. Then suddenly the scene is changed, and "the thrones were cast down, and the Ancient of days did sit . . ." (Dan. 7: 9). In words of fiery judgment the end of this present age is foretold; and then "one like the Son of man came with the clouds of heaven, and came to the Ancient of days . . . and there was given Him dominion, and glory, and a kingdom, that all people, nations, and languages, should serve Him . . ." Here is the clearest Old Testament prophecy of the One who is to receive the Kingdom. But unlike all the eager hopes of the Jews, it would be a totally different type of Kingdom from those which preceded it. It would not be a world-empire like that of Rome. He would not out-Caesar Caesar, but *be given* the kingdoms of the world by God the Father, as King of kings and Lord of lords.

That prophecy still awaits its ultimate fulfilment. In that fact we have a most important consideration concerning this name: it links together His first and second comings; it relates the first to the second, and the second to the first. We must never separate the two. Our Lord, by His self-chosen name, emphasized this essential connection of His two advents. He who came in humility is coming again in power and great glory. The second coming is the complement of the first, as the first was the essential preliminary to the second.

This being so, it is not surprising to find that Jesus used this name "Son of man" in three distinctive connections— (i) concerning His earthly ministry (Matt. 8: 20; 9: 6; 11: 19; 16: 13; Luke 19: 10; 22: 48, etc.); (ii) when foretelling His Passion (Matt. 12: 40; 17: 9, 22; 20: 18; Mark 10: 33; Luke 9: 22; John 3: 14; 8: 28; 12: 23; 13: 31, etc.); and (iii) in His teaching regarding His coming again (Matt. 13: 41; 24: 27, 30; 25: 31; Luke 18: 8; 21: 36, etc.). Of His earthly ministry He said, "The Son of man came not to be ministered unto, but to minister, and to give His life a ransom for many" (Mark 10: 45). The word "came" implies His pre-existence, His Deity; it also declares His true Humanity. He entered into our human life voluntarily, in great humility, and for a high purpose. He was, however, not merely *a* man, but *representative* man, the last Adam, the Second Man; as our Puritan forebears delighted to call Him, the Federal Head of the new creation. For "as in

Adam all die, even so in Christ shall all be made alive"
(1 Cor. 15: 22). All this is gathered up in the expressive title,
"The Son of man."

From the Gospels we leap to the Book of the Revelation—
for the only occurrence of this title between them is Acts 7: 56,
to which we have referred—and there we find our Lord once
more described as "Son of man" in His heavenly glory. But
note that here, as in Daniel 7: 13, the title is modified by the
words "like unto . . ." He is over all God blessed for ever; yet
still "the Man Christ Jesus." In the sanctuary on high "a
great high priest our nature wears." Now exalted to the throne,
our Redeemer and coming King is still in our likeness—but
that likeness transfigured with heavenly glory. He is the God-
Man, whose advent we await (see p. 164). When we see Him
we shall be like Him; for we shall be changed, in a moment, in
the twinkling of an eye; our bodies shall become like His
glorified body. He became like unto us, that we might be made
like unto Him.

CHAPTER TWENTY-FIVE

Son of God

SUPREME among the titles ascribed to, and claimed by, our Lord during His earthly ministry, "the Son of God" plainly declares His Deity: it might equally well be rendered "God the Son." It contains and expresses the most stupendous revelation of the New Testament—something entirely new and distinctive from all Old Testament teaching concerning God: that within the Godhead there is a plurality of Persons. As we have seen in the study of *Elohim*, the truth of the Trinity is dimly foreshadowed in the Old Testament, but it is not clearly revealed. The mystic fact of "God in three Persons, Blessed Trinity" awaited the unveiling given in the Person and teaching of the Son, and the outpouring and imparted grace of the Holy Spirit.

There are some critics—though not so many now as there were a few years ago—who deny that our Lord was the Son of God in any unique sense, but only *a* son of God in the way that all men are His "sons" by creation. That is untenable, however, by any honest student of the New Testament. It is true that the term "sons of God" is used of men (Hosea 1: 10) and of angels, in the Old Testament (Gen. 6: 2; Job 1: 6; 38: 7). But in the New Testament, the title "Son of God" is used of, and by, our Lord in quite a different way. In every instance the term implies that He is the one, only-begotten Son; co-equal, co-eternal with the Father (see p. 149).

At the annunciation of His birth, the angel Gabriel said to Mary concerning Him, "He shall be great, and shall be called the Son of the Highest" (literally, the Son of the Most High); and ". . . the Son of God" (Luke 1: 32, 35). In the one glimpse we have of Him during His boyhood, in the temple at the age

of twelve, He replied to the admonition of Joseph and Mary—
"Wist ye not that I must be about My Father's business?"
(Luke 2: 49). Here we have His first reference to the Father, in
terms which clearly declared a unique relationship. But "they
understood not the saying which He spake to them" (v. 50).
At the beginning of His public ministry, when baptized by
John in Jordan, the Father testified concerning Him, "This is
My beloved Son, in whom I am well pleased" (Mark 1: 11).
During His temptation in the wilderness the devil chided Him,
"If Thou be the Son of God . . ." (Luke 4: 3, 9), and as such
He triumphed over the adversary. In the Mount of Trans-
figuration, once more the Father spake from heaven, "This is
My beloved Son" (Mark 9: 7). Of the meaning of these
passages there can be no possible doubt.

This title "Son of God," and its cognates "His Son"
(John 3: 17; Acts 3: 13, etc.) and "the Son" (Matt. 11: 27;
Mark 13: 32), were often used by our Lord Himself; but unlike
"Son of David" such titles were never used in address to Him,
except by demons, who exclaimed ". . . Thou Son of the Most
High God" (Mark 5: 7; cf. 3: 11, and Luke 4: 41): they knew
who He was, and in this matter at least they spoke the truth.
In the use of these titles by Jesus, we have His explicit claim to
equality with the Father (John 10: 33–38). Indeed, His
repeated use of the term "Son" in juxtaposition to "the Father"
not only declared His relationship to the First Person of the
Godhead, but unfolded the great truth of the Trinity (Mark
13: 32; Matt. 23: 9, 10; John 3: 35; 5: 19–27; 6: 27;
14: 13). He habitually referred to God as His Father with
the implication of relationship shared by no other: He was
the "only begotten Son" (John 3: 16). He claimed unique
knowledge of the Father, and to be the revealer of Him
(Matt. 11: 27). When Peter made his great confession at
Caesarea Philippi, "Thou art the Christ, the Son of the living
God," He replied, "Blessed art thou, Simon Bar-jona: for flesh
and blood hath not revealed it unto thee, but My Father which
is in heaven" (Matt. 16: 16, 17).

Finally before Caiaphas, when the perjured testimony of the

false witnesses had come to naught, the High Priest put the prisoner on oath, and said, "I adjure Thee by the living God, that Thou tell us whether Thou be the Christ, the Son of God" (Matt. 26: 63; cf. Mark 14: 61, "Son of the Blessed"), and He replied "I am"—as "Thou hast said" in Matthew 26: 64 literally means (cf. Mark 14: 61, 62). The Jews rightly understood this reply, together with all His teaching concerning Himself, as a claim to Deity. If He were not God, then His repeated assertions were sheer blasphemy: there is no alternative to that dilemma. His adversaries saw the issue clearly— and rejected His claim, taunting Him even as He hung upon the Cross, "He trusted in God: let Him deliver Him now, if He will have Him: for He said, I am the Son of God" (Matt. 27: 43). The supreme mystery of grace is indeed that the Son of God, the Son of Man, hung there, the Just for the unjust, to bring us to God.

Since He was the Son of God, the grave could not hold Him. He burst the bands of death, and rose triumphant. God, who spake unto us, and redeemed us, in His Son, has exalted Him again to His right hand in the throne on high. "Unto the Son He saith, Thy throne, O God, is for ever and ever" (Heb. 1: 8). It is the wonder of divine grace that our God is our Saviour.

The title "Son of God" and its variants are found especially frequently in the writings of St. John and St. Paul. John tells us that he wrote his Gospel explicitly "that ye might believe that Jesus is the Christ, the Son of God" (John 20: 31); and that designation of the Lord occurs repeatedly throughout his chapters. Paul also describes Jesus as God's own Son (Acts 13: 33); and in his epistles leaves no doubt regarding the divine Sonship of Christ, using the term some sixteen times; and the writer to the Hebrews also delights to exalt the Son of God. It is interesting to note, however, that practically all these are doctrinal passages; the title is seldom used in direct address to the Lord, in ascriptions of thanksgiving and praise. As Vincent Taylor discerningly observes, "While the titles 'the Son' and 'His Son' were quite familiar to the primitive communities, they were associated with the teaching more than with the worship. The first Christians fervently believed in 'the Son' but they invoked 'the Lord.'" That is equally true to-day. We adhere unequivocally to the doctrine of the Deity of Christ enshrined in the term "Son of God," and that doctrine underlies all our worship and devotion.

CHAPTER TWENTY-SIX

Rabbi, Teacher, Master, etc.

THE MANNER in which our Lord Jesus was addressed during His earthly ministry differed, of course, with the attitude of those speaking to Him. The populace in general commonly used the honorific title "Rabbi," or its Greek equivalents "Lord," "Teacher," or "Master." The Pharisees, when they used these terms, generally did so derisively (cf. Matt. 9: 11; 17: 24). Jesus accepted the titles, however, and by His own use of them affirmed His right to all that they denoted.

(i) RABBI. An Aramaic word, meaning "my great one," this title was given by courtesy to every professed teacher of the Law. It occurs but seldom in the Gospels, however, since these were written in Greek, and the evangelists naturally translated the term into one or other of its Greek equivalents (cf. John 1: 38). Unfortunately the translators of the Authorized Version did not adopt any uniform method of rendering these various designations into English, and so the distinctions in the original are not conveyed to the ordinary reader. For instance, *Rabbi* is transliterated in John 1: 38, 49; 3: 2; 6: 25, but is translated "Master" in 4: 31; 9: 2 and 11: 8. From these references alone, however, we see that our Lord was addressed as Rabbi by His disciples, by Nicodemus, and by the people. While thus receiving the title Himself, however, our Lord warned His disciples not to do so, "for one is your teacher, even Christ" (Matt. 23: 7-12). "Christ's prohibition of the title to His disciples," says Fausset, "is against using it in the spirit of exercising dominion over the faith of others. The Triune God is the only 'Father,' 'Master,' 'Teacher,' in the highest sense; in Him alone can implicit trust be placed. All are 'brethren' before Him, none by office or precedence nearer to God than another."

(ii) RABBONI. An intensified form of "Rabbi," *Rabboni* is used only twice in the Gospels—by blind Bartimaeus, in his plea that he might receive his sight (Mark 10: 51); and Mary Magdalene, in her glad exclamation of recognition, after the resurrection (John 20: 16). It has a personal note in it— "My Teacher," "My Master."

(iii) TEACHER (*Didaskalos*). The term "teacher" occurs much more frequently in all the Gospels than *Rabbi*—though, once again, this is obscured in the A.V. by the translation "Master" in the majority of instances (cf., for example, Matt. 8: 19; 12: 38; 19: 16; 26: 18; Mark 5: 35; 9: 17; 10: 20; Luke 22: 11; John 11: 28). Jesus explicitly claimed the title (Matt. 26: 18; John 13: 14), and in a unique sense: He was not *a* teacher, but *the* Teacher. The people sensed this, "for He taught them as one having authority, and not as the scribes" (Matt. 7: 29). In His interview with Nicodemus, our Lord insisted upon this distinction. Nicodemus, having greeted Him respectfully as "Rabbi," went on to say, "we know that Thou art a teacher come from God" (John 3: 2)—which was a significant acknowledgment from the one who was recognized as "the teacher of Israel" (v. 10). But Christ would not meet him on that ground: He would not parley with him as one teacher to another. He spoke with an authority supreme and divine, and put Nicodemus in his rightful place as a very beginner and learner. Our Lord is not to be numbered among the great "teachers" of the ages: He is *the* Teacher, the Fount of all truth and wisdom. Thus we see that, as with all other titles, "teacher" became invested with a new meaning when applied to Christ: He is far above all to whom the word has ever applied, *the* Teacher come from God indeed, Himself God the Son, to lead His people to all truth.

(iv) GUIDE (*Kathēgētēs*). Occurring only once in the New Testament, this term is used by our Lord immediately following His command to His disciples not to be called "Rabbi"— "Neither be ye called masters (guides): for one is your Master,

even Christ" (Matt. 23: 10). The word is practically synonymous with "teacher," but with the further thought of the
influence which a teacher exercises in *guiding* a pupil. Our
Lord not only enlightens the minds of His disciples, but also
leads into the way of truth.

(v) MASTER. No fewer than six Greek words used concerning
our Lord are rendered "Master" in the Authorized Version!
While *Rabbei*, *Didaskalos* and *Kathēgētēs* would more exactly be
translated "teacher," there are three words rightly rendered
"Master"—but each possessing a distinctive meaning difficult
to convey in any one English word.

(a) *Epistatēs.* Used only by Luke—but by him no fewer than
six times (5: 5; 8: 24, 45; 9: 33, 49; 17: 13)—this strong term
means a chief, commander, leader, or overseer. It denotes the
Lord's absolute authority, to which the disciple is ready to give
unhesitating obedience.

(b) *Oikodespotēs.* Meaning literally "ruler of the house," this
word is translated "master of the house" (Matt. 10: 25;
Luke 13: 25; 14: 21); "goodman of the house" (Matt. 20: 11;
24: 43; Mark 14: 14; Luke 12: 39); and "householder"
(Matt. 13: 27, 52; 20: 1; 21: 33). Where these references apply
to our Lord, they refer to His authority over His disciples, the
members of His "household" through faith; and also over all
mankind, at His coming again. In story form He declared that
the destinies of men are in His hands; and that He permits
"tares" to remain in the "field" in which He has sown the
good seed of the Kingdom, until the time of the harvest: then
He will send forth the angel-reapers to gather out the tares and
burn them, while the "wheat" will be gathered into His
"barn." In that day He also will bestow rewards for service
rendered Him, according to His will. By this title, therefore,
our Lord claims supreme authority over all men, in this life,
and that to come.

(c) *Despotēs.* Twice only is this word "despot" or "ruler"
used in the New Testament concerning our Lord—and, significantly, those two instances are by Peter, foremost of the
apostles, and Jude, the Lord's brother according to the flesh

(2 Pet. 2: 1 and Jude 4, R.V.). It is a word with a rather sinister ring, in the Greek, for it means "one who has absolute ownership and uncontrolled power" (W. E. Vine), and was used of a master of slaves who exercised over them a rigid authority. Yet these two men who had been so near to the Lord, in the flesh, now delighted to call themselves His bond-slaves (for that is the Greek word translated "servant," 2 Pet. 1: 1; Jude 1), and deliberately used also this word which stressed the unquestioning obedience they delighted to render Him.

Now the fact that so many different Greek words have been rendered into the one English word "Master," while obscuring the distinctions of meaning in the original, has imparted to this word, for the majority of readers reared and nourished upon the Authorized Version, a meaning and value which, quite frankly, is not conveyed by the Greek. "Master," to most Christians of the English-speaking world, expresses the mingled aspects of our devotion to Him: it gathers up in itself something of the value of the whole range of terms we are here considering—Saviour, Teacher, Lord, Coming King, etc. The rich significance imparted to the word by its use in the Authorized Version is well illustrated in the story of George Herbert's self-dedication. Disappointed of his hopes of high office in the State, owing to the death of James I, this scion of a noble family renounced his worldly ambitions and, becoming ordained, was appointed rector of the country parish of Bemerton, near Salisbury. A distinguished company gathered for his induction, and waited at the church door while he entered alone to toll the bell—as the law then required. That duty done, he did not emerge as expected, and a friend at length looking through a window saw him prostrate on the ground in the chancel. There he pledged his life to Christ; and that night wrote a "rule of life," which included this sentence—"I beseech Him that my humble and charitable life may so win upon others as to bring glory to my JESUS, whom I have this day taken to be my Master and Governor; and I am so proud of His service that I will always observe, and obey, and do His will, and

always call Him 'Jesus, my Master.'" Afterwards he wrote
his immortal poem:

How sweetly doth "My Master" sound! My Master!
  As ambergris leaves a rich scent
    Unto the taster:
  So do these words a sweet content,
An oriental fragrancy, "My Master."

With these all day I do perfume my mind,
  My mind e'en thrust into them both;
    That I might find
  What cordials make this curious broth,
This broth of smells that feeds and fats my mind.

My Master, shall I speak? O that to Thee
  "My servant" were a little so,
    As flesh may be;
  That these two words might creep and grow
To some degree of spiciness to Thee!

Then should the pomander, which was before
  A speaking sweet, mend by reflection,
    And tell me more:
  For pardon of my imperfection
Would warm and work it sweeter than before.

For when "My Master," which alone is sweet,
  And e'en in my unworthiness pleasing,
    Shall call and meet,
  "My servant," as Thee not displeasing,
That call is but the breathing of the sweet.

This breathing would with gains by sweetening me
  (As sweet things traffic when they meet)
    Return to Thee.
  And so this new commerce and sweet
Should all my life employ, and busy me.

CHAPTER TWENTY-SEVEN

His Titles as Messiah of the Jews

THE WORD "Messiah" gathered up for the Jews of our Lord's day all their expectation and hope of a great national deliverer and leader. Their conceptions were, for the most part—as we have seen in our consideration of the title "Christ"—mistaken: but that was not the fault of the prophetic Scriptures, which they so wilfully misinterpreted. To express all that is truly conveyed by "Messiah" several titles are used in the New Testament, which present a remarkable composite picture of His Person and office, in relation to the Jewish people. Some of these have a wider application than to the Jew; but that is primary.

(i) HE THAT SHOULD COME. There was a general expectation of "one that should come," which John the Baptist expressed in the question he sent to Jesus from prison, "Art Thou He that should come, or look we for another?" Jesus gave him what was really a plain, although seemingly ambiguous, reply (Luke 7: 19–23). His words and works alike attested that He was indeed the Christ. Some three years later, the hopes of the populace were voiced in that acclamation which accompanied the triumphal entry into Jerusalem, "Blessed is He that cometh in the name of the Lord" (Matt. 21: 9). To the woman of Samaria, who had said, "I know that Messias cometh . . .," He replied, "I that speak unto thee, am He" (John 4: 25, 26). And Martha confessed, "Thou art the Christ . . . which should come into the world" (John 11: 27). These and other references emphasize that He came into the world in fulfilment of explicit prophecies given through inspired men of old; and that He came, sent of the Father, at the appointed time, and for a specific purpose—as He Himself said, "to seek and to save that which was lost" (Luke 19: 10; cf. Isa. 61: 1–3). He came forth from God, of His own will (Mark 1: 38), but according to pre-determined purpose in which He submitted His will to that of the Father (John 6: 38; Heb. 10: 7). He was the Promised One: as the Christmas hymn describes Him, "The Saviour promised long." Not all the prophetic promises were fulfilled in His earthly life and ministry, however; many anticipated also His Second Advent. So the writer to the Hebrews gives Him still the title—"*He that shall come* will come, and will not tarry" (Heb. 10: 37). The culmination of the purposes of God in Christ awaits His coming again in glory.

(ii) THE SENT ONE. In His High-Priestly prayer our Lord spoke of Himself, in address to the Father, as "Jesus Christ, whom Thou hast sent" (John 17: 3). Some critics affirm that this is a confession of inferiority to God, on the part of our Lord. That suggestion is refuted by all His teaching concerning Himself recorded in John's Gospel—to go no farther afield. Quite plainly, our Lord was referring to Himself as Man, sent forth from "the bosom of the Father" (John 1: 18) on the mission of redeeming sinful mankind.

(iii) SON OF ABRAHAM. In his genealogy of Jesus, Matthew describes Him as "the son of Abraham" (Matt. 1: 1; cf. Luke 3: 34). In His true humanity, His descent was traced from the great progenitor of the nation and "father of the faithful." Our Lord was, "concerning the flesh," an Israelite (Rom. 9: 4, 5). In that fact lies our greatest debt to the Jews (Gal. 3: 14).

(iv) SON OF DAVID. This was, to the Jews, the most cherished of all the Messianic titles, for it expressed their nationalistic ambitions. In using it they envisaged an earthly glory for Israel outstripping that of the "golden age" of David and Solomon. When addressed to our Lord in sincerity, as by blind Bartimaeus (Luke 18: 38, 39) and by the children on "Palm Sunday" (Matt. 21: 15, 16), He accepted the title: but in dispute with the Pharisees He demolished their false conceptions by pointing out that David's "Son" was also his Lord (Matt. 22: 41–45). He was not here denying that He was "Son of David"—as some critics assert—but claiming a yet greater glory, a higher dignity than earthly royalty (see p. 166). He was the Messianic sovereign; but His exercise of sovereignty would not be as they imagined. He was nevertheless the fulfilment of all their expectations—as one day the remnant of Israel will recognize (Rom. 11: 25-27). Paul, true Jew that he was, delighted to point out that our Lord was "of the seed of David according to the flesh," but he went on to exalt Him in His higher relationship and greater dignity, "the Son of God" (Rom. 1: 3, 4; 2 Tim. 2: 8).

(v) THE PROPHET. John the Baptist, asked if he were "that prophet," answered "No"—but implied that the One he heralded would be (John 1: 21, 25-27). The allusion here was to the promise of Moses, that God would raise up a prophet like unto himself (see p. 103). On several occasions our Lord was described as a prophet (John 6: 14; 7: 40); and manifestly that was how many of the people regarded Him (Matt. 21: 46; Luke 7: 16; 9: 8; 24: 19). Nor did He dispute this title: indeed, He implied its true applicability (Luke 4: 24; 13: 33). The Pharisees sneeringly rejected the idea (Luke 7: 39); but Peter, speaking in the power of the Spirit after Pentecost, declared that in Jesus was fulfilled the word of Moses (Deut. 18: 15; Acts 3: 22; 7: 37). God, who spake in time past through the prophets, spake finally in His Son: He in whom the prophecies found their fulfilment was Himself the last and greatest of the prophets. In His Person as well as in His utterances, He was God's last word to Israel, and to all men. The designation "prophet" is not used of Him in any later part of the New Testament than Acts 7: 37, however, as all that it implies finds fuller expression in other titles of Christ.

(vi) KING. We have seen that the names and titles of Christ took on a new and greater meaning than ever before, when their true significance was revealed in His Person and work. So it is with "King." Until Jesus came, no one thought of such a sovereignty as that expressed in His glorious designation, "King of kings and Lord of lords." The Jews conceived of the coming Messiah as *their* King. And such He was, and is, though in rebellion they determined, "We will not have this man to reign over us" (Luke 19: 14), because He did not conform to their ideas and lend Himself to their schemes and ambitions. He was nevertheless born King, the angel having announced to Mary that He should be given the throne of His father David (Luke 1: 32). As King of the Jews He was worshipped by the Magi (Matt. 2: 2), and acclaimed by Nathanael (John 1: 49); as such He was greeted when He entered Jerusalem in triumph (John 12: 13). The leaders of the nation spurned His claim with contempt and derision; so they made this the basis of their accusation of Him before Pilate (Luke 23: 1, 2; John 19: 12), and Pilate's examination of Him focused upon that one point (John 18: 33–39). On that charge He was condemned (John 19: 13–16), crowned with thorns (vv. 2, 3), and crucified (v. 19).

The vision of the crucified and risen Lord enthroned in the majesty on high, and in due time to come again to reign, inspired and sustained the Church from its earliest days; but the title "King" was used sparingly, as it was apt to be given a highly dangerous political implication (Acts 17: 7). Therefore the title "Lord," which could not be so easily misunderstood, was habitually used, and invested with all that "King" implies. From Pentecost onward, His people delighted to "crown Him Lord of all," and looked forward to the day when He shall be crowned with many crowns, as the kings of the earth cast their crowns at His feet (see p. 167).

(vii) JUDGE. Again with a primary application to Israel, "Judge" is a title of our Lord which signifies universal sovereignty. The ultimate source of judicial authority is God the Father (Heb. 12: 23), but He has committed the work of judgment unto the Son (John 5: 27; Acts 10: 42; 2 Tim. 4: 1). That judgment extends to every living soul—the redeemed must appear before the judgment seat of Christ (2 Cor. 5: 10), and the unsaved before the Great White Throne (Rev. 20: 11–13). Meanwhile, a process of judgment is operative here and now (John 9: 39) through the impact of His Word, and the response or otherwise of individuals to it (John 12: 48). That fact imparts a solemn responsibility upon all Christians for the preaching of the Gospel, which is to some a savour of life unto life, and to others of death unto death (2 Cor. 2: 15, 16). Thus the Messiah is accomplishing His work of mercy and of judgment, among both Jew and Gentile.

CHAPTER TWENTY-EIGHT

His Titles as Saviour

K NOWN among theologians as the soteriological titles of Christ, the group of names related to His work of redemption are most precious to all believers. Incidentally, the term "Redeemer" is never used of our Lord in the New Testament, though "redeem" and "redeemed" occur both in the Gospels and Epistles, in describing what He accomplished for sinful men by His death upon the cross (Luke 1: 68; 24: 21; Gal. 3: 13; 4: 5; Tit. 2: 14; 1 Pet. 1: 18; cf. Rev. 5: 9; 14: 3, 4). To "redeem" originally meant to pay the purchase-price of a slave, in order to set him free. So Christ "purchased" us "with His own Blood" (Acts 20: 28); we are "not our own," for we are "bought with a price" (1 Cor. 6: 19, 20). Our condemnation and penalty have been borne by our Redeemer; and our guilt is blotted out. Released from the slavery of sin and Satan, we now enjoy the glorious liberty of the sons of God (Rom. 8: 1–4). All that the word "Redeemer" means is thus set forth in the New Testament; and it is expressed also in other titles of Christ as the Saviour. Foremost among these, of course, is:

(i) SAVIOUR. In this name His relationship to His people as Redeemer is succinctly declared. It was to "save His people from their sins" that He came (Matt. 1: 21); to bear their sins in His own body on the tree, and so save them from death, the dread "wages" of sin, bestowing instead the free gifts of pardon and eternal life. This was the glad note of the angel's message to the shepherds, at His birth (Luke 2: 11). Yet, surprisingly, this name occurs but rarely in the New Testament. The two references already quoted are all that appear in the Synoptic Gospels; and in the Fourth Gospel the term is used only once—by Samaritans! (John 4: 42). In Acts, this expressive title is ascribed to Jesus by Peter, in his speech before the council—when he described Him as "exalted . . . to be a Prince and a Saviour" (5: 31); and by Paul, at Antioch (13: 23). In these two speeches the full implication of the word is deliberately emphasized. But it is not found in any of Paul's epistles to *Churches*. How, it might be asked, can we explain this seeming avoidance of so important a title, which so aptly sums up the very essence of the Gospel? In reply, it has been suggested that this reticence is due to the fact that the Roman emperors claimed—among their other grandiose designations—the title of "saviour of the world." The apostles would naturally wish to avoid any misunderstanding on the part of their readers, or possible involvement with the authorities.

In the pastoral epistles, however, we have a striking use of the term, for it is there applied to *God the Father* (1 Tim. 1: 1; 2: 3; 4: 10; Tit. 1: 3; 3: 4); and this repeats the phrase of the Virgin Mary, in her *Magnificat* (Luke 1: 47). Mary was, of course, adapting a term often found in the Old Testament; and her use of it, together with Paul's at a later date, emphasizes that the salvation of men was the work, not of our Lord Jesus only, but of the Trinity. "God was in Christ, reconciling the world unto Himself" (2 Cor. 5: 19). The best known text in the Bible, John 3: 16, stresses the fellowship of the Father and and Son in the redemption of sinners. Perhaps we seldom realize that it cost the Father as much to give His Son, as it cost the Son to give His life "a ransom for many." Our only worthy response is expressed by Jude: "To the only wise God our Saviour, be glory and majesty, dominion and power, both now and for ever. Amen."

(ii) THE LAMB OF GOD. All the wealth of Old Testament symbolism in the sacrifices of the patriarchs and of the Mosaic Law invests this title with a significance out of all proportion to the infrequency of its use in the New Testament. It was John the Baptist who first applied it to Jesus, in his dramatic proclamation, "Behold the Lamb of God, which taketh away the sin of the world" (John 1: 29, 36). In these words he declared our Lord to be the sin-bearer: the one anticipated and foreshadowed in every sacrifice offered in obedience and faith. It is arresting that the Baptist should have declared at the very outset of our Lord's ministry that He had come to die; to "take away the sin of the world" (John 1: 29, 36). The apostles failed to grasp this until after the Resurrection; but our Lord, confronting the Cross, had plainly said, " . . . for this cause came I unto this hour" (John 12: 27). The great truth of substitution—the bearing of the sinner's guilt and penalty by another, qualified by perfection of being to take the sinner's place, and so becoming his "substitute"—is carried over in this metaphor from the Old Testament teaching, and made an integral part of the Gospel.

The phrase does not occur elsewhere in the Gospels, however; and only once in Acts—8: 32, where Philip quotes Isa. 53: 7 in his conversation with the Ethiopian eunuch. But the truth it expresses runs throughout the New Testament, in other titles of Christ, and in such terms as atonement, propitiation, the blood of Christ, etc. In the last book of the Bible, however, the name is used again—no fewer than twenty-six times! Our Redeemer, the One who died on the cross, in our place and stead, bearing our sin, is now our exalted Saviour, in the midst of the throne (Rev. 5: 6). That is the guarantee of the absolute accomplishment of all His purposes in the redemption of His elect.

(iii) PROPITIATION. Not strictly a title of Christ, perhaps, the term "propitiation" is applied to Him by St. John, in his first Epistle (2: 2). A better translation of the Greek word, some think, is "expiation." The allusion is to the mercy seat, and the whole doctrine of the atonement which it symbolizes. The thought underlining the apostle's words is, that Jesus is the One by whom we are made nigh to God—through His sacrifice on the Cross, and its atoning efficacy. The cleansing, forgiveness, and "covering" of sin are all implied in the term. The particular value of this passage lies, however, in the fact that John describes our Lord, not as having *accomplished* the great work of propitiation for us, but as *being* the propitiation for our sins. In a word, Atonement is not merely a doctrine, or transaction, but—Christ Himself, in all that He is and has wrought for men. Dr. Griffith Thomas emphasized, in the title of one of his books, that "Christianity is Christ." That is the cardinal fact of the Gospel, underlined in this unusual term. "By Him let us draw near . . ."

(iv) THE WAY, THE TRUTH, AND THE LIFE. Of all the titles which refer to our Lord's relationship to His people, this is the most comprehensive (John 14: 6). Not strictly a soteriological title, we include it in this section because it embraces all that He is and does as the Saviour, the reconciler of sinful men to God.

(a) He is *the Way* to the Father: the *only* way, His categorical affirmation most plainly infers. He does not say that He prepares or makes a way, but that He *is* the way. It is an awesome thought that only those "in Christ" truly know God and are known of Him. What an impetus this should give to our preaching of the Gospel and support of missions! The selfsame thought is contained in His description of Himself as the door (see p. 153). "No man cometh unto the Father, but by Me." And He does not cease to be "the way" when we are converted: ever we come unto God by Him; ever He leads us in the way everlasting.

(b) *The Truth*. He is absolute truth; the Fount and Standard of truth. The particular application of the term in this title, however, is that He is the truth *concerning the Father*: the revealer of the Father. Knowing Him as only the Eternal Son can, He makes the Father fully known to His disciples (v. 9). "No man knoweth the Son but the Father; neither knoweth any man the Father, save the Son, and to whomsoever the Son will reveal Him" (Matt. 11: 27). All that we know of God, we know in Jesus.

(c) *The Life*. Like the previous terms in this composite title, this word is used of Christ *in relation to His people*. It does not so much declare that He is Himself the Living One—as He is (Rev. 1: 18)—but that He is the *Source of (spiritual) life* to His people. He is, of course, the Source of all life. But in the new covenant He has become also the giver of eternal life (John 10:

28; 17: 2, 3). And this He gives, not as something apart from Himself; a gift He has to bestow. He *is* the life: the "eternal life," John calls Him (1 John 5: 20). It is in union with Him, that His people have everlasting life. "This life," says John again, "is in His Son . . . He that hath the Son, hath life" (vv. 11, 12).

We can but touch upon the fringe of this unfathomable subject, and indicate only the dominant thought in each of these three pregnant words. Perhaps we can do no better than to quote the prayer of Erasmus:

> O Lord Jesus Christ, who art the Way, the Truth and the Life, we pray Thee suffer us not to stray from Thee, who art the Way, nor to distrust Thee, who art the Truth, nor to rest in any other than Thee, who art the Life. Teach us by Thy Holy Spirit what to believe, what to do, and wherein to take our rest. For Thine own Name's sake we ask it. Amen.

(v) THE LAST ADAM, THE SECOND MAN. St. Paul divides the human race into two groups—those "in Adam," and those "in Christ" (Rom. 5: 12–21; 1 Cor. 15: 22, 45–49). All who are "in Christ" were once "in Adam," but made the eternally momentous transfer from the one category to the other, through faith in Jesus as their Saviour. This great transaction was possible because Christ was the last Adam, the Second Man (1 Cor. 15: 45, 47). As the last Adam, He bore the iniquities of Adam's sinful race; as the Second Man, He is the Federal Head of redeemed mankind. "In Him the sons of Adam boast more blessings than their father lost." Through Adam, sin entered into the world, with its consequences of sin and death (Rom. 5: 12, 16). In Christ, sin was judged and put away; and "the free gift came upon all unto justification of life" (v. 18). As Adam's seed, we all are "of the earth, earthy"; but in Christ, "we shall bear the image of the heavenly" (1 Cor. 15: 49). These titles embrace, then, the whole range of our salvation in Christ, from regeneration to ultimate glorification.

(vi) THE RESURRECTION AND THE LIFE. Closely akin to the final clause in "The Way, the Truth and the Life," this title, which our Lord claimed for Himself—in talking with Martha, before the raising of Lazarus (John 11: 25)—has the added thought of the ultimate triumph of His grace in us, in the "redemption of our body" (Rom. 8: 23). He who died for our sins and rose again for our justification assures His people of bodily resurrection (1 Cor. 15: 21, 22). He has triumphed over death, not only in His own Person, but on behalf of His people (John 5: 25-29; 6: 39-54). He is the Firstfruits of them that slept (1 Cor. 15: 20). His resurrection is the guarantee of ours.

(vii) THE AUTHOR (or PRINCE) OF LIFE; and AUTHOR OF SALVATION. Using a Greek word which eludes exact rendering into English, Peter describes our Lord as "the Prince of life" (Acts 3: 15); but the margin gives "Author" in place of "Prince." In 5: 31, he uses the same word in declaring Jesus to be "a Prince and a Saviour." In Hebrews 2: 10 and 12: 2, however, the same word is rendered respectively, "*Captain* of salvation" and "*Author* and Finisher of our faith." Moffatt prefers "Pioneer" in every instance. The underlying thought in these references is that life, salvation, and faith come from Christ; and He in sovereign grace associates Himself with His people in the outworking of every aspect of their salvation. He does not "save" and then leave the saved to their own devices: He *perfects* what He begins. He not only imparts His manifold grace in salvation, but both *goes before* and is present with His people, their Leader and all-sufficient Friend. Our confidence rests upon no powers of persistence of our own: He will lead and sustain through all life's pilgrimage, and at last "present us faultless before the presence of His glory with exceeding joy" (Jude 24). To such grace our response, like that of St. Paul, should be—"I know whom I have believed, and am persuaded that He is able to keep that which I have committed unto Him against that day" (2 Tim. 1: 12).

CHAPTER TWENTY-NINE

His Titles as the Christ of God

LIKE THE many facets of a jewel, each making its contribution to the brilliance and beauty of the gem, integral to it and in perfect relationship to the whole, the names of Jesus are numerous and varied; and each is indispensable to the perfection of the divine revelation of our Lord in His Person and work. It is difficult to classify some of the names, however; their meaning cannot be confined to one subject-heading. The grouping in these chapters is made for reason of convenience and not with any suggestion that the titles are limited to the scope of the general heading. Here we consider some which tell of Him as God Incarnate—the Christ of God (Luke 9: 20), in the widest implication of that term.

(i) THE WORD. Used only by St. John, the title *Logos* or "the Word" conveys most expressively the mission of Jesus as the revelation—or revealer—of the Godhead. It declares, first, His absolute Deity; and then, that in Him the full and final self-revelation of God is given (John 1: 1–18). By means of words, the thoughts and intents of the mind and heart are revealed to others; and in the Person of the Word Incarnate God makes Himself fully known. Nothing that man could possibly know about God is withholden: in Christ the divine self-revelation is complete and ultimate. "God who . . . spake in time past unto the fathers by the prophets, hath in these last days spoken unto us in His Son" (Heb. 1: 1, 2). Only One who was Himself God, co-equal and co-eternal with the Father, could make Him fully known. He came forth from "the bosom of the Father" to "declare" Him—literally, "show Him forth" (John 1: 18). A distinct Person from God (the

Father), He yet is God; and became incarnate for man's salvation (vv. 1, 2, 12–14). Here the doctrine and fact of the Trinity are presented—that there is a plurality of Persons in the one Godhead. This is a mystery of the divine Being transcending human thought, yet spiritually apprehended through the revelation given in the Son and by the Spirit.

> Thou art the everlasting Word,
>   The Father's only Son;
> God manifestly seen and heard,
> And heaven's beloved One . . .

Whether or not John was influenced by the philosophical speculations of Philo, is outside the scope of our present study. We prefer, however, to find the origins of his thought in the Old Testament, where the Word of God is His Agent in creation and in the revealing of His will to men. As Westcott says, "The Word, before the Incarnation, was the one source of many divine words: and Christ, the Word Incarnate, is Himself the Gospel." John, under the inspiration of the Spirit, wrote the profoundest truths concerning the Person and ministry of "the Word," not only in the prelude to his Gospel, but also in his first Epistle (1: 1; 5: 7), and finally in Revelation 19: 13 (see p. 168). The same thoughts underlie Paul's teaching in Colossians 1: 15–20; and see also Hebrews 1: 1–3.

(ii) THE BELOVED. Occurring only once as a title of Christ, "the Beloved" (Eph. 1: 6) expresses the love of the Father for the Son, to which many passages testify. At our Lord's baptism, the Father declared Him to be "My beloved Son" (Matt. 3: 17); and Jesus repeatedly affirmed that "the Father loveth the Son" (John 3: 35; 5: 20, etc.). This love found its highest expression in the fellowship between the Father and the Son in the "plan of salvation" of sinful men. "Therefore doth My Father love Me," our Lord declared, "because I lay down My life . . ." (John 10: 17); and in His High Priestly Prayer He prayed that the disciples might "know that Thou . . . hast loved them, *as Thou hast loved Me*" (John 17: 23). What a stupendous thought, that the Father loves those who are "in

Christ" even as He loves His beloved Son! This title, then, is full of comfort to the believer, who is "accepted in the Beloved."

(iii) THE CHOSEN OF GOD. Found in the Authorized Version only in Luke 23: 35—in the taunt of the Jews as Jesus hung upon the Cross, "Let Him save Himself, if He be the Christ, the chosen of God"—this title occurs also, in the Greek, in the audible testimony of the Father on the Mount of Transfiguration, "This is My Son, My chosen" (Luke 9: 35, R.V.). The word means "elect," and refers back to Isaiah 42: 1, "Behold My servant, whom I uphold; mine elect (chosen) . . ." —the fore-ordained, the sent-one from God (see p. 108). In fulfilment of the eternal counsels, He came forth from God to do the Father's will, in the redemption of men (Heb. 10: 7–10). He proved Himself indeed the "chosen of God" in enduring that bitter taunt, when He could have summoned ten legions of angels to deliver Him and to destroy His tormentors. But He was "chosen" unto the Cross—and the glory that should follow!

(iv) THE HOLY ONE. There is in this title a development of meaning such as we have seen in other instances. The primary thought in the word "holy" is "consecrated" or "set apart," but as applied to Jesus it speaks also of His spiritual and moral perfections. At the annunciation Gabriel spoke to Mary of the "Holy Thing which shall be born of thee," manifestly referring to the Deity of the One who was to be born her Son (Luke 1: 35). He alone of all Adam's race was "holy, harmless, undefiled, separate from sinners" (Heb. 7: 26). Demons declared Him to be the "Holy One of God" (Mark 1: 24); and Peter, speaking for all the disciples, said, "We have believed and know that Thou art the Holy One of God" (John 6: 69, R.V.). He did not mean by this that Jesus was merely a "saint," as we use and understand that term—one like themselves, only with a greater degree of sanctity: Peter was indisputably ascribing to Jesus a unique perfection in His character and a unique position in relation to God. The apostle had a yet fuller comprehension of the meaning of "the

Holy One," however, when he used the same term concerning Jesus after Pentecost (Acts 3: 14); and in Rev. 3: 7, He is called ". . . holy . . . and true . . ." Our Lord was indeed "consecrated" unto the Cross: "for this cause came I unto this hour" (John 12: 27); but only as the *Holy One* could He be a ransom for many.

(v) THE RIGHTEOUS ONE. As "holy" refers to character, so "righteous"—or "just," as the word is often translated in the A.V.—describes conduct. The two titles are intimately related: it is impossible for one to be true without the other. The term "righteous" was applied to Jesus by Pilate's wife (Matt. 27: 19), and by the centurion who crucified Him (Luke 23: 47): but in these instances, the word means merely that they had formed that impression of Him. The word "just" was used in fullness of understanding by Peter, and by inspiration of the Spirit, in Acts 3: 14 and 7: 52; and by Paul in 22: 14. Peter tells us that Jesus died "the righteous for the unrighteous, that He might bring us to God" (1 Pet. 3: 18, R.V.). His was a perfect human life. The untiring scrutiny of the Pharisees could find no deviation from absolute rectitude in His conduct. In thought, word and deed, He never departed from the standard of God's requirement and Law. He was able to challenge His accusers, "Which of you convinceth Me of sin?" (John 8: 46). Thus He proved Himself the "Lamb without blemish and without spot" (1 Pet. 1: 19), who on that account was able to be our sin-bearer. Truly He was the fulfilment of the prophecy, "By His knowledge shall My righteous servant justify many (i.e., 'make many righteous'): for He shall bear their iniquities ('unrighteousnesses')" (Isa. 53: 11). This leads to the thought that Christ, the Righteous One, is also *our righteousness* (1 John 2: 1). Our Advocate on high is the answer to all unrighteousness in His children. He is truly *Jehovah-tsidkenu* (see pp. 85-8).

> Thou hast fulfilled the Law,
>   And we are justified:
> Ours is the blessing, Thine the curse;
>   We live, for thou hast died.

(vi) THE IMAGE OF GOD. All the many titles of our Lord, together, cannot fully convey the glory of God in His Son, the visible image of the invisible God. Attempt is made to express in human language the inexpressible glory of His Person. Perhaps nearest to the mystical wonder and majesty of it, is the title "the Image of God" (2 Cor. 4: 4; Col. 1: 15; Heb. 1: 3). In Him, we see and know God.

The words "image" and "likeness" are often regarded as practically synonymous. But "image" means far more than "likeness." Sometimes a son or daughter is described as "the very image" of a parent—but really the "likeness" is superficial; they are quite different people, with different characters, however closely they may resemble one another. There is not mere similitude between God and Christ, however, but absolute one-ness. The figure of speech lying behind the word "image" is that of the impress which a seal makes in the wax into which it is pressed—a perfect representation. Jesus is the very expression of the Being of God; the outshining of His glory. "He that hath seen Me," He said, "hath seen the Father" (John 14: 9). All that God is, He is in Christ.

> In Thee most perfectly expressed,
> The Father's glories shine;
> Of the full Deity possessed,
> Eternally divine!

There is no further revelation of God—nor will there be through all eternity—than that which we have received in Christ: for there is nothing of His glory and grace unrevealed (2 Cor. 4: 6). That does not mean that we have comprehended all! We shall continue eternally to make new discoveries of the length and breadth and depth and height of the glory of God in Christ. For in Him all the fullness of the Godhead dwells (Col. 2: 9). And the surpassing wonder of redeeming grace is this: that as Jesus is the image of God, so shall His people be conformed to *His* image in the age to come (1 Cor. 15: 49; cf. 2 Cor. 3: 18; Rom. 8: 29).

(vii) THE EFFULGENCE OF THE DIVINE GLORY. In this sublime title, the writer to the Hebrews expresses the supernal glory of

Christ as the "brightness" or "outshining" of the divine Essence (1: 3). He is the embodiment of the *Shekinah*. Isaiah had foretold a day when "the glory of the LORD shall be revealed . . ." (40: 5), and the fulfilment came in Christ. "We beheld His glory," John wrote; "the glory as of the only begotten of the Father, full of grace and truth" (John 1: 14). During His Incarnation that glory was veiled; but the writer to the Hebrews endeavours to express the inexpressible glory which was His from eternal ages as the Second Person of the Blessed Trinity, and now is manifested in His glorified human body, in the throne on high—the Man Christ Jesus, our Saviour and great High Priest.

(viii) LIGHT. As the phrase "the effulgence of His glory" describes what Christ is in His own Person, in relation to the Father, so "the Light" is an associated title, regarding His relationship to mankind. "God is light," says the apostle (1 John 1: 5), endeavouring to convey in human language the transcendent glory and holiness of God. In order to bring the light of the knowledge of God to those in the darkness of sin, He who was from all eternity the visible manifestation of that unutterable glory, became Man; and as such He was "the Light of the world" (John 8: 12; 9: 5. Cf. Matt. 4: 16; Luke 2: 32; John 1: 4–9). This title, like others we have considered, stresses that He is the sole revealer of God: all true revelation, both before and during His Incarnation, was in and from Him—and it is so still, through the ministry of the Spirit. Once more the apostle is careful to indicate that it is not so much His message, but *Himself* that is the light (John 1: 4–9). There is no true knowledge of God apart from Him; nor is it enough to know *about* Him. The *life* was the light . . . "Darkness," John affirmed, "comprehended it not" (v. 5). Only those who have received from Him the gift of life can comprehend the light. Having received both life and light, however, His people are commissioned to shine forth! He who is "the Light of the world" said, "Ye are the light of the world" (Matt. 5: 14, 16)—not *sources* of light, as He is, but allowing His light to shine out from the new life within.

(ix) THE LORD OF GLORY. The One who, in the glory, is from all eternity Lord. Not only so: He is the One "to whom glory belongs as His native right" (T. C. Edwards). Nor did He cease to be such when He became "the Friend of publicans and sinners": it was the *Lord of Glory* who was crucified (1 Cor. 2: 8). In Jesus we, like the apostles of old, behold the glory as of the only begotten of the Father. James, indeed, explicitly declares Him to be—

(x) THE GLORY (Jas. 2: 1). Note that the words "the Lord of" in the A.V. and R.V., in this text, are in italics, indicating that they are not in the Greek. James, brother of Jesus according to the flesh, who did not believe on Him during His public ministry, here makes the unequivocal declaration that He is the *Shekinah*: the visible manifestation of God. John likewise, endeavouring to express the inexpressible, calls Him the—

(xi) ONLY BEGOTTEN (John 1: 14, 18)—"the idea conveyed by which," says Warfield, "is not derivation of essence, but uniqueness of relation; so that what is declared is that beside Jesus Christ there is no other: He is the sole complete representation of God on earth." Moreover, He is also—

(xii) THE FIRSTBORN. The eternally only-begotten Son became the Firstborn by His resurrection, St. Paul declared at Antioch, quoting Psalm 2: 7 as his authority (Acts 13: 33). The same thought is repeated in Romans 1: 4. Our Lord had accomplished the purpose for which He became man, and assumed once more His position and prerogatives as the Son of God. But He was raised and exalted as the Redeemer of men: the One who had put away their sin, and become the Federal Head of the new creation. Through His death and triumphant resurrection, He is "bringing many sons unto glory" (Heb. 2: 10). "As in Adam all die, even so in Christ shall all be made alive" (1 Cor. 15: 22). He is the "Firstborn among many brethren" (Rom. 8: 29). It is true that in Colossians 1: 15 He is described as "the Firstborn of every creature," for "by Him were all things created"; but Paul goes on to add, "He is the Head of the body . . . the Firstborn from the dead" (v. 18). He who was the Agent of God in creation is the "Firstborn" of the new creation (see p. 162). His "brethren," however, are "sons" of God by adoption, through His grace: He is *the* Son of God, by eternal Being and right. Our "elder Brother" is our Lord and our God. He is—

(xiii) HEIR OF ALL THINGS. As the Firstborn, Christ is, the writer to the Hebrews affirms, the Heir of all things (Heb. 1: 2). This is, in effect, only another way of emphasizing His unique Sonship. He takes rank over all created beings, and His inheritance embraces the universe, unto all eternity. It would seem presumption to add, if it were not so clearly stated in the Word, that He has made His redeemed to be sharers of His glory: to be "heirs of God, and joint heirs with Christ" (Rom. 8: 17). His glory is matched by His grace.

Thus, under many titles, the inspired writers present the One who "left His throne and kingly crown" to be born in a stable and laid in a manger; who went about doing good, and who hung upon a cross—for love of you and me.

> Were the whole realm of nature mine,
>   That were an offering far too small:
> Love so amazing, so divine,
>   Demands my soul, my life, my all.

CHAPTER THIRTY

His Titles as Head of the Church

ETWEEN the titles of Christ which set forth His Person
and work as Saviour, and those which declare Him to
be the Head of the Church, there is no sharp dividing
line; for the functions of our Lord in these two capacities merge
one into the other. As soon as a person is saved, he becomes a
member of the Church; and the Christ who saves is the Head
of the Church. Some of the titles which follow might therefore
well apply to both capacities.

(i) BRIDEGROOM. First used concerning Christ by John the
Baptist (John 3: 25–30), this title is rich in significance. Most
obviously, John intended it to imply that Jesus was the Messiah.
Equally clearly it had that meaning on the lips of our Lord
Himself (Mark 2: 19, 20). But the choice of this word, by both
the Baptist and Christ, meant more than that: for the metaphor
of husband and wife was steeped in Old Testament association,
being frequently used concerning the relationship between God
and Israel (cf. Isa. 54: 5; Jer. 31: 32; Hos. 2: 1–23). "The use
of 'the Bridegroom' as a designation of our Lord assimilates
His relation to the people of God to that which in the Old
Testament is exclusively, even jealously, occupied by Jehovah
Himself" (Warfield). But our Lord went on to speak, seemingly
so strangely in this context (Mark 2: 20), of His being "taken
from them"—a plain allusion to His death. He was indicating
that the perfect relationship expressed in this figure of speech,
never realized in the experience of Israel through their sin and
folly, would be brought about in Christ, and by His death. Our
Lord expanded this theme in His parables of the ten virgins
(Matt. 25: 1–13) and the marriage of the King's son
(Matt. 22: 1–14): in these He stressed that eternal destiny

is determined by relationship to Himself. He opens and shuts the door, and the one qualification for admission is to be "known" of Him; the invitation goes out unto all, but those admitted must have on the wedding garment of His providing.

St. Paul takes up this metaphor, in 2 Cor. 11: 2, where he writes of having "espoused" them "unto one husband, that I may present you as a chaste virgin to Christ"; and it is implied in his references to the Church as the Bride of Christ (Rom. 7: 4; Eph. 5: 25–32). Finally, in the Apocalypse, the consummation of the purposes of God in the realized union of Christ and the Church, is described under the vivid imagery of the "marriage of the Lamb" (Rev. 19: 7; cf. 21: 9; 22: 17). In this title, therefore, the wonder and grace of the relationship with the Lord into which He will finally bring His redeemed people, is most graphically set forth.

(ii) SHEPHERD. We have seen that in the Old Testament this figure of speech expresses the most tender aspect of the relationship between God and His people *individually* (pp. 81–4). While that thought is carried over to the New Testament, the metaphor of the shepherd is also enlarged to apply to His people as a *flock*. Our Lord used it first, naturally, concerning Israel—speaking of the people as "sheep not having a shepherd" (Mark 6: 34); and "the lost sheep of the house of Israel" (Matt. 10: 6; 15: 24). Their rejection of Him becoming manifest, however, He indicated His rejection of the nation, and the establishing of a new, spiritual "Israel." This He did when he addressed His disciples as a "little flock" (Luke 12: 32)—the nucleus of the "many" whom He would gather from many nations, that they might become "one flock," having "one shepherd" (John 10: 16, R.V.). After His resurrection He assumed this relationship to His Church, in His commission to Peter (John 21: 15–17). Thus He is described by the writer of the Hebrews as "the great Shepherd of the sheep" (Heb. 13: 20), and by Peter as "the Shepherd and Bishop of our souls" (1 Pet. 2: 25). This title, then, conveys alike the loving care of the Lord for His people individually and communally.

He never neglects the one in His concern for the many; but He would bring all into true relationship with one another—which is realized in a true relationship to Himself.

(iii) DOOR OF THE SHEEP. It might seem at first glance that the title of the Lord as the *Door of the Sheep* (John 10: 7, 9) should be classified among those which emphasize His work as Saviour. "I am the door," He said; "by Me if any man enter in, he shall be saved." Here our Lord stresses, as Peter did after Him, that "there is none other name under heaven given among men, whereby we must be saved" (Acts 4: 12). There is no other way into the "fold," no other way of becoming a member of His "flock," than by believing on the Lord Jesus Christ: no other way into the Kingdom, than *through* Him. But faith in Christ unto salvation is not the end and fullness of His purpose for His elect. Regeneration is but the beginning of a life not only of fellowship with Him, but also of service for Him. So our Lord went on to say, ". . . shall be saved . . . and shall go in and out, and find pasture." "The door is not for use once only," says Westcott, "that we may gain admittance into safe precincts and then lie down in idle peace, but for that daily going out and coming in which sums up the activity, the influence, the growth of the Christian." And the IVF Commentary observes, "Jesus is the door, a door of entrance and exit; a door by which we obtain access into the Father's presence (14: 6), and through which we pass into liberty, life and service."

Interpreting our Lord's words thus, Bishop Westcott goes on to say that "the fold, which the Christian enters through Christ, the fold which gives safety to the flock, is a place for shelter and not a place for isolation." He takes the words, "shall go in and out" to mean the necessary contacts of Christians with the world; indeed, our deliberate "going out" among the unsaved, in order to witness and maybe lead them into the fold. "Therefore it is that the Christian goes forth, as his Lord opens the way, to claim fresh victories for the Faith." And *in so doing*, the "saved . . . find pasture." Therein lies a fundamental principle: that the spiritual life is nourished and strengthened, not in cultivating it as an end in itself, but in a fellowship of service with and for the Lord. It is not the cloistered life, but the most fruitful, that is the most spiritual.

(iv) MEDIATOR. Volumes have been written upon the mediatorial work of Christ—as on other subjects touched but lightly in these studies. We can only indicate in broadest outline the Scriptural teaching concerning this title. Not that the word "mediator" occurs often in the New Testament: on the contrary, it is applied to Christ only four times. Yet the truth it expresses underlies all divine revelation concerning Him. St. Paul sums it up in a sentence—"There is one God, and one mediator between God and men, the man Christ Jesus" (1 Tim. 2: 5). Jesus is, he declares, the answer to the longing of the heart of man, expressed in agonized words by Job, "How can a man be just before God? . . . there is no daysman betwixt us, that might lay his hand upon us both" (Job 9: 2, 33, R.V.). Someone to bridge the gulf between the all-holy God and sinful man! Moses, pleading with God for idolatrous Israel; and Abram, for the cities of the plain—these are faint adumbrations of the mediatorial office: but they were intercessors rather than mediators. Our Lord alone could "lay His hand upon . . . both," for the essential qualification of a mediator is that He should be both God and man—and Jesus alone fulfils the condition. Only one who is truly man can stand in our behalf before God; and only one who is Very God can be His representative in mediatorial grace toward erring men. The very use of the word "man" by St. Paul, in the phrase "the man Christ Jesus," conveys that He is not merely a man: He is the one who, "being in the form of God," was made "in the likeness of men" (Phil. 2: 6, 7), and having "borne our sin in His own body on the tree" (1 Pet. 2: 24) now is enthroned, in our human likeness, glorified, "the one mediator between God and men." He who died for our sins, and was raised again for our justification (Rom. 4: 25)—

Pursues in heaven His mighty plan,
The Saviour and the friend of man.

The writer to the Hebrews adds the specific thought of Him as "the mediator of the new covenant"—the one who brought into being the new ground of relationship to God, in place of the Law (Heb. 8: 6; 9: 15; 12: 24). This embraces the whole range of New Testament teaching concerning the setting aside of Israel and the Mosaic covenant, and the establishment of the Church, redeemed and made nigh to God by His blood. While the word "mediator" has therefore, perhaps, primarily a soteriological connotation, it cannot be limited to Christ in His work and office as Saviour: it envisages His ministry as Advocate and High Priest; and it includes within its purview the entire Church.

(v) ADVOCATE. Closely related, in the thought of most Christians at least, to "mediator," is the word "advocate" or "paraclete," used by John concerning our exalted Lord—"If any man sin, we have an advocate with the Father, Jesus Christ the righteous" (1 John 2: 1). It is the same word as Jesus used concerning the Holy Spirit, translated in the Authorized Version "the Comforter" (John 14: 16; see p. 181). There, in speaking of "*another* paraclete," our Lord implied that He Himself was such to His disciples. The word conveys the thought of all that He *was* to the Twelve, and all that He *did* for them. Literally, *paraclete* was a technical law term, meaning "a friend at Court." As used by our Lord here, however, it can be invested with the opposite meaning—"a Friend from Court," bringing grace from on high. John, of course, in his Epistle, employs the word in its usual meaning: when we sin, we have a "Friend at Court" to plead our cause. But, as Vincent Taylor trenchantly says, "It would obviously be wrong to suppose that by the phrase 'an Advocate with the Father' he means that, through His intercession, Christ moves the Father to be gracious toward sinners. As the Father, God is gracious already and always. The idea can only be that, as our Paraclete, Christ identifies Himself with us and speaks for us, voicing our penitence and our longing for reconciliation with God."

This raises the question which perplexes many, concerning the relationship between the Father and the Son within the unity of the Godhead; but for our purpose, the teaching of the text is, simply, that the believer is reconciled unto God in Christ, in all the range of his need on the one hand, and of the Lord's redemptive work, on the other. His merits avail for us, in our shortcomings as Christians equally as in our regeneration. He, and His worth, are the answer to every accusing voice, and every thought and word and deed of ours which would bring us into condemnation. He is "Jesus Christ the righteous," not only in Himself, but as our representative: He has "fulfilled the Law" on our behalf, and His righteousness is imputed to us (Rom 4: 22–24). The advocacy of Christ, therefore, does not constitute of *pleading* on our behalf every time we sin: His very presence before God is the full and sufficient answer to our need. In Him we have forgiveness; and in Him we are presented unto the Father.

(vi) HIGH PRIEST. Only in the Epistle to the Hebrews is Christ directly designated a High Priest: but in it, this is the central theme. The writer is at pains both to liken and to contrast the High Priesthood of Christ with that of Aaron. While the Person and the work of Christ were foreshadowed in Aaron, He both transcended and superseded the Levitical Priesthood. He fulfilled all that was typified in it, and in so doing abolished the Mosaic order. He entered, not the Most Holy Place of the earthly sanctuary, but heaven itself (Heb. 9: 7–24), bearing, not the blood of goats and calves, but His own blood, by which He obtained eternal redemption for His people (v. 12). Thus He fulfilled absolutely all that was prefigured in the supreme ceremonies of the tabernacle and temple, and the most exalted functions of the High Priest—those of the great day of Atonement. In a word, our Lord Jesus Christ has, by His death and resurrection and ascension, made "whosoever will" among guilty sinners "nigh unto God."

Not only is Jesus—who according to the flesh was not a member of the priestly family of Aaron—superior to Aaron on these accounts: the writer of the Epistle affirms also that His High Priesthood is of quite a different order—i.e., that of

Melchizedec, who was king-priest of Salem (Gen. 14: 18–20; Heb. 5: 5–10; 6: 20–7: 28). His is a royal priesthood; it is His by right of His eternal Sonship, untransmitted and intransmissible (Heb. 7: 16–24). Withal, He exercises it in virtue of His true Humanity: it "became Him to be made like unto His brethren" (2: 14–18). Having as Man put away our sin, He now is our representative and intercessor in heaven (9: 24). This two-fold aspect of His work on our behalf—that accomplished during His Incarnation, and that continuing in the glory on high—is expressed by the writer in the graphic phrase, "the Apostle and High Priest of our confession" (3: 1, R.V.)—the One who was *sent forth* by the Father to accomplish our redemption, and now applies its benefits and ensures its out-working in our experience.

The writer of the Epistle makes all this teaching the ground of a powerful plea for faith and love toward the Lord on the part of all his readers. Christ has "full atonement made," and has opened for us the way into the holiest of all, so that we may draw near with boldness, knowing that our God is our Saviour (4: 14–16; 7: 23–28). He knows all our frailty and weakness, and is ready and able to help in every time of need. He, if we will trust and obey, will lead us into the fullness of the purpose and provision of God (10: 19–39).

Although the term High Priest is not applied to Christ elsewhere in the New Testament, there are allusions to His High Priesthood—it is implied, for instance, in Rom. 8: 34 and 1 John 2: 1; and in the vision granted to the seer on the Isle of Patmos, He is described as wearing a High Priestly garment, together with a royal girdle (Rev. 1: 13). Thus the last glimpse of Him permitted to human eyes after His ascension and before His return, presents Him as the King-Priest, yet in our likeness: our Saviour and our God.

(vii) THE STONE. A figure of speech somewhat more obscure than most, that of the Stone is adopted by New Testament writers—following the example of our Lord Himself—from several Old Testament Scriptures, notably Psalm 118: 22; Isaiah 8: 14; 28: 16; Daniel 2: 34. These passages imply a cataclysmic divine judgment, first upon Israel, and ultimately upon the godless nations, establishing in their place the Kingdom of God. Our Lord quoted Psalm 118: 22 in the parable of the wicked husbandmen (Mark 12: 10); and Peter followed His example, in his speech before the Sanhedrin (Acts 4: 11). In both instances the meaning is plain: Jesus, being rejected by the nation through its leaders and representatives, became the "keystone" of a new "spiritual house" which would take the place of dispossessed Israel. That thought underlies the majority of the references to Christ as the Stone. He is the "corner stone" of the spiritual temple, the Church, which replaces the temple in Jerusalem, and all it represents (Eph. 2: 19–22). Scholars are not agreed whether the Greek word used here means "top-stone" or the basic corner stone which binds together the foundation and the walls: in either case the allusion to Christ is the same—He is the One upon whom the whole edifice depends. Of this "temple," all who are "saved" through faith in Jesus (Acts 4: 11) are "living stones" (1 Pet. 2: 5; Eph. 2: 21, 22). St. Paul deliberately mixes the metaphors of building and growing, to emphasize that there is nothing mechanical about the up-building of the Church: it is the growth of a living organism, a *spiritual* temple. This is the practical outcome of faith in Christ, of unity with Him. In contrast, to those who reject He is a stone of stumbling and rock of offence: the One who divides between men—unto life, or death. This is true of individuals, and of nations (Matt. 21: 43, 44; Rom. 9: 31–33; 1 Cor. 1: 23).

Closely related to this title is that of Christ as the ROCK, smitten and riven (1 Cor. 10: 4), from whom the life-giving water of salvation flows (see p. 28).

(viii) THE TRUE VINE. Found in the New Testament only in John 15: 1, 5–8, the metaphor of the vine is adapted by our Lord from its use in the Old Testament, where it is a symbol of Israel (Psa. 80: 8–19; Isa. 5: 1–7; Jer. 2: 21; Ezek. 15: 1–8; 17: 6–10; 19: 10–14; Hos. 10: 1). In all these references, however, the allusion is to *apostate* Israel; and the context is of judgment. That probably is why the Lord described Himself in John 15 as the *true* Vine—the adjective is emphatic in the original, which reads, "I am the Vine, the true." This is another indication of the setting aside of Israel and establishing of the Church. He would bring His redeemed people into such relationship to Himself as would fully realize the purposes of God. An intimacy so complete as to be true one-ness is symbolized. As Vincent Taylor points out, Christ does not say He is the stem, but the vine—the very life of His community. His people are "in" Christ; and He in them (v. 4). "Abiding" in Christ is the secret of fruit-bearing (v. 5); and by fruit-bearing alone God is glorified in His people, and His heart satisfied (v. 8).

(ix) HEAD OF THE BODY. Whereas the metaphor of the Vine emphasizes the one-ness of Christ and His Church, the apostolic teaching concerning Christ as Head of the Body is a salutary reminder that the exalted Lord is supreme and distinctive, "over all, God blessed for ever" (Rom. 9: 5). The one-ness is as clearly presented as under the simile of the Vine; but the unique position and glory of the Lord is also stressed (Rom. 7: 4; 12: 4, 5; I Cor. 12: 12–27; Eph. 1: 22, 23; 4: 15; 5: 23; Col. 1: 18; 2: 19). Again, as in the case of every metaphor concerning Christ and the Church, the sacred writers make clear that there is nothing mechanical in the obedience of the Body to the Head; "as the Head Christ rules, but His commands are operative only in the obedience of the members of the Body" (cf. Rom. 7: 6; 12: 1–3; Eph. 4: 1–3, etc.). Nevertheless, the Church is His "fullness" (Eph. 1: 23); but "this does not mean that Christ, or His revelation, is imperfect, but that He limits His activity by the living medium of its expression" (Vincent Taylor). His people are united to Him in His Humanity; yet He in His own Person is the eternal Son of the Father, the Second Person of the Triune Godhead. There is therefore danger of misunderstanding and error in referring to the Church by such phrases as "the extension of the Incarnation."

The wondrous relationship here set forth needs, indeed, no extravagances to magnify it! Here is grace beyond all human imagining; here is a mystery—as Paul rightly described it (Eph. 5: 32); yet a mystery revealed by the Spirit, to the quickened spirit. Here is a relationship with the Lord in which we rejoice—with wondering awe, and adoring worship.

(x) THE LIVING BREAD. In His discourse to the people who came thronging eagerly around Him on the day following the feeding of the five thousand, our Lord described Himself as the Bread of Life—and they were perplexed and displeased (John 6: 35–59; 61). He contrasted Himself with the manna which God had given to the children of Israel in the wilderness: He would satisfy the *inner* man; and not for an hour or two only, but for ever. Some expositors link this teaching with the Sacrament of Holy Communion (1 Cor. 10: 17), but therein lie obvious dangers. Both passages refer to the life supplied and sustained by the Crucified and Risen Lord.

In these several titles, therefore, the intimacy of relationship which every member of the Church enjoys with its exalted Head, is set before us; and the sufficiency of His grace to meet every need of His children, both for everyday personal life, and for service unto Him.

CHAPTER THIRTY-ONE

Apocalyptic Titles

MID THE rich symbolism of the Book of Revelation is a
profusion of names and titles of Christ, many highly
figurative—in keeping with the character of the Book—
which together present a wondrous picture of our Lord, in
the splendour of His Person and the illimitable riches of His
grace. As we would expect in the final Book of the Bible, the
total revelation concerning Christ, given here a little and there
a little throughout the preceding Scriptures, is gathered up in
the composite "portrait" of Him here presented. Here we
behold the majesty of His Being—so far as it can be expressed
and comprehended this side of the Veil; the manifold offices
which are His, as the eternal Son who became Man for us men
and our salvation, and now is God-Man on the throne; and the
ultimate glory of His consummated purposes, in eternal union
with His redeemed—His Bride.

It would seem that the writer, under the inspiration of the
Spirit, added title to title in his endeavour to express the inexpressible; as if by the cumulative effect of these he might
convey something of the ineffable glory of the exalted Lord—
which no heart can fully conceive, or tongue tell. Often these
titles, like a gem with many flashing facets, reveal different
aspects of His glory and grace—as God, Saviour, High Priest,
or Judge. To tabulate and discuss them separately would
destroy much of their significance; for it is their juxtaposition
one with another that imparts the full value. So we shall
glance at them as they appear in the Book, and also in relation
to one another.

In his brief introduction the seer describes the book as "the
Revelation of JESUS CHRIST"—the personal name and official

title joined together; this had become the most commonly-used designation of the Lord, in the early Church, displacing the single name "Jesus" of the Gospels. John goes on to describe Him as " *the faithful witness, and the first begotten of the dead, and the prince of the kings of the earth* " (1 : 5). "The triple title applied to Christ corresponds to the three ideas of the Book—Christ the Revealing Prophet, the Life-giving High Priest, and the real Ruler of mankind" (Ellicott's Commentary).

(i) FAITHFUL WITNESS. He who, as the eternal Son, alone knows the Father, came to reveal Him (Matt. 11 : 27); and in this title John affirms that our Lord indeed fulfilled that purpose. He was the faithful witness "not only in respect of this revelation, but as concerning the whole truth of God" (IVF Commentary). John's first emphasis, at the very beginning of his "revelation of Jesus Christ," is that He came from the Father, to make Him fully known: and that *He perfectly did so.*

(ii) FIRST BEGOTTEN OF THE DEAD. Others before Jesus had been raised from the dead: but none *unto eternal life*; none as the life-giving One (1 Cor. 15 : 45; Col. 1 : 18). In this arresting phrase, the apostle declares that He has triumphed over death, as Man, in order to share that triumph with man (see p. 142). Those who are "dead in trespasses and sins" can find eternal life in Him—and in Him alone: which means that the eternal destiny of all mankind is in His hands.

(iii) PRINCE (or, RULER) OF THE KINGS OF THE EARTH. Absolute sovereignty is claimed for Him—and that, not only in the age to come, but *now*: He *is* the Ruler of the kings of the earth (Rom. 13 : 1). The whole "Revelation" foretells His future dominion over all: but it also underlines the teaching of the entire Scriptures, that even now He is "Lord of all" (Acts 10 : 36). It is by Him that kings reign; and He is, through all the tangled web of human history, effecting His sovereign will.

Here we have a three-fold picture almost blinding in its splendour, and awe-inspiring in its claims. It is well for us that John goes on to say that this glorious One is also " *He that loved us, and washed* (or, as the word should probably be correctly translated, 'loosed') *us from our sins in His own blood.*" This gathers up the various soteriological titles: He is the Saviour, who so loved us that He shed His own precious blood for our redemption.

At the beginning of the Apocalypse proper, John tells how he heard the voice as of a trumpet, saying, "I am—

(iv) ALPHA AND OMEGA, THE FIRST AND THE LAST" (1: 11). This is one of several titles ascribed in this Book both to God the Father and to Christ (1: 8; 2: 8; 21: 6; 22: 13), emphasizing the Deity of our Lord. "It is probable that the phrase translates for Greek readers the Hebrew idiom whereby the first and last letters of the Hebrew alphabet were used to express the entirety of a thing. . . . Here the meaning is that God is the Lord of all history, its beginning and its end, and the whole course between" (IVF Commentary). The oldest MSS. omit it, however, from 1: 11.

Like all the other names we are considering, *Alpha and Omega* sets forth not only what our Lord is in Himself, but also what He is *to usward* who believe. He who is the First and the Last, is *our* eternal, unchangeable Lord. By this title He revealed Himself to John as the One who moves in sovereign authority among the lampstands—representing the Church in its completeness and diversity (Rev. 1: 11). It does not mean merely that He is eternal, but also the Lord of history—and especially in relation to His people. From the past eternity unto the ages to come, He is working His purposes out. In all the generations of men He accomplishes His good will.

The eternal Son of the Father, in His Incarnation, entered our finite life in order to lift us up out of the realm of the finite into His eternal purpose and Kingdom. By His grace we fallen creatures receive, through faith, the gift of everlasting life, and the assurance of eternal inheritance among the saints in light (Col. 1: 12; Heb. 9: 15). We become members of His Church. This title gives the guarantee that He who has begun a good work in us will perfect it (Phil. 1: 6). He is the end *of faith*, as its beginning. He is Alpha and Omega, in His own Being, and in His grace toward His elect.

Turning to "see the voice" that spoke with him, John beheld the seven golden lampstands, and in the midst, one like unto the—

(v) SON OF MAN, clothed with a garment down to the foot, and girt about the paps with a golden girdle. His head and his hairs were white like wool, as white as snow; and His eyes were as a flame of fire; and His feet like unto fine brass, as if they burned in a furnace . . . (1: 13–15). This vision of the King-Priest amid His church, is of surpassing glory. It is a vision, indisputably of God; yet of God "like unto a Son of man"—for how else shall John tell of Him who is God and Man, God-Man; in our human likeness, yet glorified? The vision recalls those of Daniel (7: 9; 10: 5, 6), for the exalted Lord combines both the Danielic "Son of man" and "Ancient of days"—His true Humanity is united to His essential Deity. In this one designation His priestly ministry, His divine majesty, His omniscience, and His work of judgment within the Church, are graphically portrayed (see pp. 120–2).

Having given this preliminary pen-portrait, John takes phrases from it, and uses them in his introductions to the messages to the seven churches, presenting different aspects of the Lord's Person and purpose, according to the needs of the various churches. He has left no doubt in the mind of any enlightened reader that Jesus Christ is *God the Son*, and *Son of Man*; that He is the *Saviour*, and *Head of the Church*—this last relationship to His people dominates chapters 2 and 3. He who walks, as Lord, in the midst of the seven golden lampstands, holds the "stars"—the "messengers" or ministers—of the Churches in His hand: signifying absolute authority to dispose of each according to His will (2: 1).

In the message to Smyrna, His Deity as the *First and Last* is linked with His Saviourhood: *which was dead and is alive*—repeating 1: 17. He who possesses eternal life as the Second Person of the Godhead submitted to death, and triumphed over it in the behalf of sinful men; and is alive for evermore, the Saviour and author of life to all who believe.

To Pergamos, He is—

(vi) HE WHICH HATH THE SHARP SWORD WITH TWO EDGES—signifying judicial authority (2: 12). It is an inflexible principle of Scripture that "judgment must begin at the house of God" (1 Pet. 4: 17). The sword has, however, two edges, "so as to convict and convert some (vv. 13, 17), and to convict and condemn others" (vv. 14–16) (JFB).

To Thyatira, He is "*the Son of God, who hath His eyes like unto a flame of fire, and His feet like fine brass*" (2: 18; cf. 1: 14, 15). Again the emphasis is upon His penetrating discernment and His judicial function *within the professing Church*.

To Sardis, He is—

(vii) HE THAT HATH THE SEVEN SPIRITS OF GOD, and the seven stars (3: 1). Seven, in Scripture, is the number of perfection. The phrase "the seven Spirits of God" is variously interpreted by expositors as meaning: (a) the Spirit in His fullness; (b) the Spirit in the perfection of His operations; or (c) perfect spiritual endowment (cf. Isa. 11: 2, 3; Rev. 5: 6). This phrase is highly symbolic, expressing the absolute perfection of the Spirit in all His attributes and activities (see p. 177). In relation to the Church, He is the Gift of Christ (1 Pet. 1: 11; John 15: 26; 16: 7); so here our Lord is described as "He that hath the seven spirits of God"—fullness of resource to meet every need of the seven "stars," and of all His people.

In the message to Philadelphia, two titles stressing His Deity are joined to one which is Messianic: He is—

(viii) HOLY—an attribute which can be predicated of God alone (see p. 145);

(ix) TRUE—"Jesus is 'true' in the sense of 'true to His Word,' *i.e.*, faithful" (IVF Commentary). "His nature answers to His name," observes Fausset. These two terms are applied to God in Rev. 6: 10.

(x) HE THAT HATH THE KEY OF DAVID: He that openeth, and no man shutteth; and shutteth, and no man openeth (3: 7). This presents Him as the Messiah, the fulfilment of Old Testament expectations and prophecies. The "key of David" is a clear reference to Isaiah 22: 22. He alone has authority to admit whom He will into the Kingdom (see p. 166).

To Laodicea—which some expositors consider to be especially representative of the Church at the end of the age—He is the:

(xi) AMEN. His is the final word in any matter, in every issue, over every life. He is Himself "God's seal of His own word" (JFB); "the Guarantor and Executor of the declared purposes of God" (IVF Commentary). He is also the *Faithful and True Witness*—see (i). He is the One who has borne true and full testimony concerning God, and His will and purpose for men; He has fully revealed the Father. It is not for lack of knowledge that any to whom the Gospel of Christ has come will perish.

(xii) THE BEGINNING OF THE CREATION OF GOD (3: 14). "Better translated 'the principle' or 'source' of creation" (IVF Commentary). He by whom and for whom all things were created, and in whom all things consist (Col. 1: 16, 17) in great humility seeks to win the love and loyalty of sinful, rebellious creatures of His hand!

Son of God; Son of Man; Revealer of the Father; Redeemer of men; Holy, True, Faithful; yet judging His people, and admitting whom He will into His Kingdom—this is the *Head of the Church*, which these two chapters present.

From chapter four onwards, the scope of the Book widens, to embrace the heavens and earth and hell; time and eternity; and we behold the Lord in further capacities and relationships. First, the seer is given a vision of the throne of God (4: 1-3), and the challenge goes forth, "Who is worthy to open the (seven-sealed) book, and to open the seals thereof?" (5: 2). To which reply is made, "The—

(xiii) LION OF THE TRIBE OF JUDA, THE ROOT OF DAVID . . ." (v. 5). These are among the Messianic titles most cherished by the Jews, summing up all their national aspiration. The lion is the symbol of strength and sovereignty. Israel's supreme glory will be realized, however, not as they thought, through *a* son of David who would "out-Caesar Caesar," but by *the* Son of David who was also David's Lord (Matt. 22: 41-45). This title, like certain others we have considered, is not only Messianic but millennial; it not only declares His Kingship, but His Deity.

Seeking to behold this majestic personage, John saw a—

(xiv) LAMB. The Greek word is not that generally used for lamb, but a diminutive, "little lamb"—a term of endearment, equivalent to "a precious lamb" (Fausset). This one word gathers up in itself all the titles of Christ as Saviour (see p. 138); and by joining together the most emphatic and inclusive Messianic and soteriological titles, John unites Jew and Gentile in Christ: he indicates His purposes for both, in redeeming grace (John 11: 49–52). The lamb "newly slain" (v. 6) is yet the lamb "slain from the foundation of the world" (13: 8) in the purposes and will of God: the Cross was no after-thought, but was pre-determined before all ages—so greatly did God love mankind, whom He purposed to make in His own image and likeness. The lamb, however, is not here a figure of weakness; He who "was led as a lamb to the slaughter" now has "seven horns"—symbolic of absolute power, the horn representing authority (Psa. 75: 4–7) and royal dignity (Zech. 1: 18–21); and "seven eyes"—representing omniscience: perfect knowledge and perception. The Lamb is, indeed, the Lion of the tribe of Juda. Not only so: He is—

(xv) KING OF KINGS AND LORD OF LORDS (19: 16; cf. 17: 14). He is, indeed, the King eternal, immortal, invisible (1 Tim. 1: 17); but this Book is dealing with His purposes concerning this earth: and here the seer once again declares His absolute sovereignty, which shall be manifested and exercised in all the range of its implication at His Second Coming. To Him every knee shall bow; and every tongue shall confess that He is Lord, to the glory of God the Father (Phil. 2: 10, 11). Indeed, this is another title applied both to God and to Christ; for in the great doxology at the close of 1 Timothy, St. Paul says of God, in arresting words, "Who is the blessed and only Potentate, the King of kings, and Lord of lords; who only hath immortality, dwelling in the light which no man can approach unto; whom no man hath seen, nor can see: to whom be honour and power everlasting" (1 Tim. 6: 15, 16). This glory and sovereignty will be manifest in the Son, at His appearing. To those who have in this day of grace rendered Him a glad obedience, acknowledging Him King in willing submission and unfeigned love, that day will hold no terrors; for the King of kings is also the—

(xvi) WORD OF GOD (19: 13). The One "who, being in the form of God, thought it not a thing to be grasped after to be equal with God; but made Himself of no reputation, and took upon Him the form of a Servant, and was made in the likeness of men"—in order to bring us the glad message that "God so loved the world that He gave His only begotten Son, that whosoever believeth in Him should not perish but have everlasting life." (For a fuller treatment of this title, see p. 143.) To all who "believe" He has become the—

(xvii) BRIGHT AND MORNING STAR (22: 16). The one who "ushered in the day of grace" (JFB) will also "lead up the dawn of everlasting day" (Ellicott's Commentary). We look for His Coming as men who look for the dawn.

What a galaxy of names and titles! What a Lord and Saviour they present! What a revelation of Jesus Christ! The Lord of Glory, our Redeemer and Coming King. Even so, come quickly, Lord Jesus!

> Join all the glorious names
>   Of wisdom, love, and power,
> That ever mortals knew,
>   That angels ever bore:
> All are too mean to speak His worth,
> Too mean to set my Saviour forth.

Part III

NAMES AND TITLES OF THE HOLY SPIRIT

The things of God none knoweth, save the Spirit of God—1 Corinthians 2: 11, R.V.

"What does the great variety of names by which the Holy Ghost is known in the New Testament, import? One thing is, the fullness of revelation about Himself in the Word, each name telling us something more than the rest of what He is. Indeed, were there nothing more told than His names, we should have in them alone a rich revelation concerning Him. Another thing which these names set before us is our own spiritual need, in its unspeakable depth and breadth, and His blessed sufficiency to meet that need on all sides. For every one of these names has a practical bearing on our souls"—J. ELDER CUMMING.

"The distinctive glory of the dispensation of the Spirit is His divine personal indwelling in the heart of the believer, there to reveal the Father and the Son"—ANDREW MURRAY.

CHAPTER THIRTY-TWO

The Spirit of God

THE FACT that God is "Three in One" is not revealed—although it is implicit—in the Old Testament. The Spirit of God was regarded therefore not as a Person of the Godhead, but as *God in action* by His Spirit. The Hebrew word translated "Spirit" lent itself to this point of view: it is, elsewhere rendered "wind" and "breath." As the wind is invisible and inexplicable, yet possessing vital power, experienced alike in gentle breeze or mighty tornado, so the Spirit was regarded as God in His mysterious operations. Our Lord used that very figure of speech (John 3: 8). "Breath" contains the further thought of the "spirit of life." God, having fashioned man out of the dust of the ground, "breathed into his nostrils the breath of life; and man became a living soul" (Gen. 2: 7).

The first reference to the Spirit is found in Genesis 1: 2, in relation to creation. After the calamity which marred the original creation, so that the earth became without form and void, "the Spirit of God *brooded* upon the face of the waters"— it is the word used of a mother hen, cherishing her chicks. Out of the ugliness of ruin was brought, by the Spirit, the beauty and order we enjoy in the earth. The great work of restoration, like the initial creation, was wrought by the Three Persons of the Trinity: by the word of the Father (Heb. 11: 3); in and through the Son (Heb. 1: 2); and by the Spirit (Gen. 1: 2). The Psalmist declares the Spirit's activity in creation (Psa. 33: 6) and in all the processes of nature (104: 30). God has not left the world merely to the outworking of laws and principles; He sustains and orders all things by His Spirit, so that indeed there is a real sense in which we may "see God in nature."

Our present concern, however, is His dealing with mankind. The first reference to the Spirit in relation to men is stern and challenging, and sums up the story of sin and degradation preceding the Flood: "My Spirit shall not always strive with man" (Gen. 6: 3). Next comes a striking contrast: the testimony of Pharaoh concerning Joseph—"a man in whom the Spirit of God is" (Gen. 41: 38). Now Pharaoh was a heathen, and probably thought of the "Spirit of God" in terms of his mythological beliefs: but nevertheless his statement was profoundly true, though he uttered more than he knew. Pharaoh recognized in Joseph a wisdom and "spirit" which distinguished him from the wisest and most exalted of his Egyptian counsellors. Thus we find, so early in the divine revelation, the Spirit of God imparting gifts and graces which were on a higher level than the noblest natural endowments.

A further most suggestive stage in the Biblical teaching on the Spirit is reached in Exodus 31: 3, where Bezaleel is "filled with the Spirit of God, in wisdom, and in understanding, and in knowledge, and in all manner of workmanship," to supervise the preparation and construction of the tabernacle. He was manifestly a genius: an artist and highly skilled craftsman. But over and above these natural gifts, the Spirit of God came upon him to impart especial ability for the task to which he had been appointed. That is deeply significant. We often think of "Spirit-filled" men and women as the outstanding prophets and saints: but the Spirit comes not only to give inspired words to the preacher, but also skill and enablement to ordinary folk in the everyday avocations of life.

During the troubled period of the Judges, we read of the Spirit of God coming upon one after another, to deliver and judge His people—Othniel, the godly son-in-law of Caleb, upon whom He came and remained for forty years (Jud. 3: 10, 11); Gideon, with whom He "clothed Himself" (6: 34, margin), so that it was not so much Gideon as the Spirit of God in and through him who wrought the mighty works; Jephthah (11: 29) and Samson (14: 6, 19; 15: 14), whose stories emphasize the unimaginable grace and longsuffering of God in His dealings with men.

Next in the story of the Spirit's empowering is Saul, who was so manifestly filled with the Spirit that he prophesied (1 Sam. 10: 6, 10); but all too soon we read of his defection, until ultimately the Spirit departed from him (16: 14). Of his successor, however, we are told that "the Spirit of the LORD came upon David from that day forward" (16: 13).

A summing-up of all this history of God's dealings with His people by His Spirit is given in Nehemiah 9: 20, 30—"Thou gavest also Thy good Spirit to instruct them . . . and testified against them by Thy Spirit in Thy prophets . . ." And so we are introduced to the prophets, who uttered the oracles of God by the Spirit. In one such utterance, Joel foretold the "outpouring" of the Spirit at Pentecost (Joel 2: 28; Acts 2: 16). Micah, contrasting the bounteous resources of God with the sorry condition of the people, asked, "Is the Spirit of the LORD straitened?" and went on to demonstrate what they all might have experienced if they would—"But truly I am full of power by the Spirit of the LORD . . ." (Micah 2: 7; 3: 8). Finally Zechariah, speaking regarding the restoration of the temple, laid down an abiding spiritual principle governing all work for God—"Not by might, nor by power, but by My Spirit, saith the LORD of hosts" (Zech. 4: 6).

In the New Testament, the unveiling of the Personality of the Spirit is one of the major themes; but the persisting use of the term "the Spirit of God" indicates the continuity of His work, and links the fuller New Testament revelation with all that had been given in the Old.

When sending out the Twelve on their mission, our Lord foretold that they would be "brought before governors and kings for My sake," and exhorted them to "take no thought how or what ye shall speak . . . for it is not ye that speak, but the Spirit of your Father which speaketh in you" (Matt. 10: 18–20). After His resurrection He told them to wait in Jerusalem for "the Promise of the Father" (Acts 1: 4). The most significant passage, however, is 1 Corinthians 6: 11, "But ye are washed, but ye are sanctified, but ye are justified in the name of the Lord Jesus, and by *the Spirit of our God.*" The words "washed . . . sanctified . . . justified . . ." embrace our entire experience in the Christian life, from regeneration to full Christian maturity—and all is effected through the redemption wrought *for* us by Christ, and *made effectual in our experience* by the Spirit. He it is who takes of the things of Christ, and reveals—unveils and imparts—them unto us (John 16: 15). All that we are and have in Christ is ours in and by the Spirit of God.

St. Paul writes of the Corinthian believers as "our epistle written in our hearts . . . not with ink, but with *the Spirit of the living God*" (2 Cor. 3: 3); and St. Peter, speaking of the "fiery trials" through which some of his readers were called to pass, encouraged them with the thought that "*the Spirit of glory and of God* resteth upon you" (1 Pet. 4: 14). That is a worthy final enlargement of this O.T. title for the Third Person of the Trinity. "The Spirit of glory" contains the promise of glory for all the redeemed: for at the appearing of our Lord these bodies of our humiliation shall be changed into the likeness of the body of His glory—and in that transfiguration the work of the Spirit of God in men will find its ultimate fulfilment.

CHAPTER THIRTY-THREE

The Spirit and the Believer

As a great number of names are needed to express the glory and grace of God the Father, and of our Lord Jesus Christ, so several names are ascribed to the Third Person of the Trinity. These include the titles we have glanced at; also others which express His essential Deity, His attributes, His ministry among men, and the gifts He bestows.

The truth of "God in Three Persons, Blessed Trinity" was revealed, as we have seen, only in and through the Person and ministry of Christ. The revelation of the Son was given in His coming to be our Saviour. He, in turn, imparted the revelation concerning the Personality and coming of the Spirit, whom He promised to His disciples (John 14–16). In these words of the Lord we have the clearest, most explicit teaching regarding the Spirit. The *Paraclete* would, He stated, be to the disciples what Jesus Himself had been to them—and more, for He would be in them; indeed, by the indwelling of the Spirit, both the Father and the Son would dwell in them (John 14: 23). The Spirit would glorify Him (Jesus), as He had glorified the Father (John 16: 14). All New Testament revelation concerning the Spirit, then, relates to the operation of God among men unto the glorifying of Christ and the fulfilling of the Father's will. All that the Holy Spirit is revealed to be, *He is in relation to mankind, and especially the people of God.* He it is who makes real in our experience the gifts and callings of God in Christ. All true spiritual experience, from conviction of sin to conformity to Christ, is by the Spirit. Every gift of God, every operation of grace, is *in* Christ and *by* the Spirit. He presents

to men the claims and virtues of Christ; and every response of
faith on our part is by the Spirit.

> And every virtue we possess
> And every conquest won,
> And every thought of holiness
> Are His alone.

It is very difficult, if not impossible, therefore, to differentiate
between the gifts and grace of Christ, and those of the Spirit;
indeed, the selfsame operations are attributed both to Christ
and the Spirit. "Thus," says Bishop Moule, "the believer
'lives by the Spirit' (Gal. 5: 25), and 'lives by faith in the Son
of God,' who 'lives in him' (Gal. 2: 20). The Spirit 'dwells in
him' (1 Cor. 3: 16) and 'Christ dwells in his heart, by faith'
(Eph. 3: 16, 17; cf. Rom. 8: 9-11). The Spirit 'sanctifies'
him (1 Pet. 1: 2), and Christ 'is made unto him sanctification'
(1 Cor. 1: 30)."

So, first, we see that the Spirit—the "Spirit of God" (Matt.
3: 16; 1 Cor. 6: 11; 2 Cor. 3: 3) is also, in relation to men—

(i) THE SPIRIT OF CHRIST (Rom. 8: 9) and

(ii) THE SPIRIT OF JESUS (Phil. 1: 19). He is, says Moule, "the
Spirit of Christ in the work of redemption. . . . He who testifies
of Christ, and glorifies Him, does this not only as His holy
Messenger and Co-operator, but as the Stream of love and life
from Him the Fountain." "The general idea of the Johannine
teaching," observes Griffith Thomas, "is that the departure of
Christ was to issue in the gift of the Holy Spirit, as the special
bestowal of the new covenant for the purpose of perpetuating
Christ's spiritual presence and effecting His redeeming work.
Thus the Holy Spirit would at once be a revelation of truth, a
bestowal of life, and an equipment for service." In one very
interesting passage, Romans 8: 9, the Spirit is called both "the
Spirit of God" and "the Spirit of Christ"—"showing the
equality and functions of the one Godhead. The Father is the
source of all grace; the Son, the channel; the Spirit, proceeding
from the Father and the Son, the agent" (IVF Commentary).
Albeit, the Spirit must never be regarded as merely an "agent"

in the modern usage of that word: He is no "subordinate"
representative of the Godhead, but is—

(iii) THE LORD THE SPIRIT (2 Cor. 3: 18, R.V.). This title,
which is incorrectly rendered "the Spirit of the Lord" in the
A.V., gives the Third Person of the Trinity the designation
which is the New Testament equivalent of *Jehovah*, and is
ascribed to God the Father, and to our Lord Jesus Christ. Its
reference here to the Holy Spirit bears witness to His essential
Deity, and co-equality with the Father and the Son. "The
Holy Spirit," Griffith Thomas writes, "is closely related to
God (Rom. 8: 9); is regarded as possessing personal activities;
and is intimately bound up with Christ (Rom. 8: 9). The
activity of Christ as the Redeemer and Head of the Church is
regarded as continued by the Holy Spirit, and yet with all this
intimacy of association they are never absolutely identified."
Another title often cited as applying to the Holy Spirit is—

(iv) THE ETERNAL SPIRIT (Heb. 9: 14). The exegesis of this
text is disputed, however. Westcott—among other scholars—
renders it, ". . . Christ, who through His eternal Spirit offered
Himself . . .," and comments, "The absence of the article from
pneuma aiōnion marks the spirit here as a power possessed by
Christ, His 'Spirit.' It could not be said of any man absolutely
that his spirit is eternal; but Christ's Spirit is in virtue of His
Divine Personality eternal. . . ." So, while the adjective
"eternal" might truly be applied to the Spirit, this verse does
not strictly relate to the Third Person of the Godhead. The
fact that the Holy Spirit is eternal is implicit, however, in all
the Scriptural teaching concerning Him.

In the Book of Revelation, John uses a title which has caused
some perplexity—

(v) THE SEVEN SPIRITS OF GOD (Rev. 1: 4; 3: 1). As we have
seen elsewhere (p. 165), this title expresses the completeness of
the Spirit's perfections, operations and gifts. There is no
warrant in this highly symbolic title for any teaching which
violates the Personality of the Spirit as the Third Person of the
Trinity. Paul distinctly affirms that He is—

(vi) ONE SPIRIT (Eph. 4: 4). In all the varied names by which

He is revealed, and in His manifold ministries among men, He is "one Spirit"—the Spirit who came upon Jesus in bodily form, like a dove, and now dwells in *our* hearts.

Coming to the names which indicate more specifically both His personal qualities and the gifts He bestows upon men, He is, first and foremost—

(vii) THE HOLY SPIRIT (Matt. 1: 18; 28: 19). This, indeed, is His characteristic name, both in the New Testament and in the language of the Church. Holiness is, in the Bible, predicated of God alone: but He wills that men also should be holy—"Be ye holy, for I am holy"—and has sent forth His Spirit to make this possible. So the Holy Spirit is also—

(viii) THE SPIRIT OF HOLINESS (Rom. 1: 4). Every attribute of the Spirit is a promise of grace to the believer. What we are not, and cannot be of ourselves, we may become through grace: for God has given us His Spirit, the Spirit of Jesus, to make us holy. This He does by applying the efficacy of Christ's redeeming work, in cleansing and delivering us from sin; and by "working in us to will and to do of His (God's) good pleasure" (Phil. 2: 13; Heb. 13: 21). Christ, who is "made unto us sanctification" (1 Cor. 1: 30) abides in us by His Spirit (Gal. 2: 20): all the holiness we can ever know is the very life of Christ in us, in the power of His resurrection (Phil. 3: 10). Holiness in everyday life, then, is not a matter of "the best we can be and do," but rather is the work of God in us by His Spirit, the Spirit of holiness. The secret lies in the oft-repeated phrase, "not by striving, but by trusting . . ."

Another aspect of the character and ministry of the Spirit is revealed in the title—

(ix) THE SPIRIT OF WISDOM (Eph. 1: 17). Elsewhere Christ is said to be "made unto us wisdom" (1 Cor. 1: 30). Our Lord is the fulfilment of the Old Testament personification of Wisdom (see p. 101). Once again we see that what Christ is said to be to His people is true also of the Spirit. And how reassuring is that fact! We are so often conscious of our foolishness and limited understanding. But James exhorts us, "If any of you lack wisdom, let him ask of God . . ." (Jas. 1: 5). That, it need scarcely be said, is not a promise of sudden intellectual brilliance! It is certainly true that the Holy Spirit does illumine the mind: but His function is to reveal and glorify Christ, "in whom are hid all the treasures of wisdom and knowledge" (Col. 2: 3). In knowing Christ, we know ultimate truth. The more we know of Him, the more we know of the true wisdom, not of this life only, but of eternity. To lead into the full knowledge of the Lord Jesus is the supreme ministry of the Spirit. This is indicated also in the closely-related title—

(x) THE SPIRIT OF TRUTH (John 14: 17; 16: 13). Christ declared Himself to be ". . . the truth" (John 14: 6); and the Holy Spirit is "the Spirit of truth" in revealing Jesus. He leads into the understanding of the written Word—of which He is the author—and enables the reader to see "beyond the sacred page" the Incarnate Word. That, in itself, would not be enough, however; we must not only *comprehend* but *apprehend*. Truth is not merely veracity and rectitude: an abstract standard of belief and conduct, which we see exemplified in the life on earth of Jesus of Nazareth. *The truth* is the very life of Christ in its perfections, in contrast to the perversions of the "father of lies" (John 8: 44); and the Spirit of truth is given to impart to the believer the very character, the very life, of Christ Himself. To that end He is—

(xi) THE SPIRIT OF FAITH (2 Cor. 4: 13). Faith is the one factor in our salvation, the one quality in us which God requires, in response to the redemption He has provided in Christ: and of that *we cannot boast*, for it is *not of ourselves*, but is a gift of God, by His Spirit (Eph. 2: 8). But again we must stress that faith is not just a mere *gift*: it is an activity of God in the heart, by His Spirit. And the Spirit who quickened faith in us unto salvation will lead us "from faith to faith" (Rom. 1: 17): the life begun in an act of faith continues in a constancy of faith. And for every need, every demand of this life of dependence, God has given us "the Spirit of faith." He is, moreover—

(xii) THE SPIRIT OF GRACE (Heb. 10: 29). This sums-up the titles which declare the working of God in men: all is comprehended in the one word "grace." Out of His divine bounty,

God bestows gifts upon men (John 1: 16). Unmerited favour! And every gift of grace is ministered to us by the Spirit. The Spirit of grace is the Spirit of the God who so loved the world that He gave His only begotten Son, and who "with Him, freely gives us all things" (Rom. 8: 32); who delights to give, even as a Father to His children. For such we are, by grace through faith: for the Spirit is—

(xiii) THE SPIRIT OF ADOPTION (Rom. 8: 15). In the experience of the new birth, we have become members of the family of God; the Spirit bears witness with our spirit that we are children of God (Rom. 8: 16), and quickens within our hearts the cry "Abba, Father" (v. 15). To this we were predestinated (Eph. 1: 5); but the eternal calling and election of God was made effectual in our experience by the Spirit (see p. 95). And the Spirit of adoption, who leads us into this privileged relationship, is thus—

(xiv) THE SPIRIT OF YOUR FATHER (Matt. 10: 20). And so the cycle is complete! Every good gift cometh from God (Jas. 1: 17), who has blessed us with all spiritual blessings in heavenly places in Christ (Eph. 1: 3); and these blessings become ours by the Spirit, who delights to glorify Jesus, to gratify the Father, and to enrich His people. But the full story is not yet told: the total of the names and titles of the Spirit is not yet reached. Further revelation of the riches of His grace is contained in yet other names. He is also, for instance—

(xv) THE SPIRIT OF LIFE (Rom. 8: 2; Rev. 11: 11). The truth contained in this title has already been anticipated; but it is doubly assuring to have it explicitly stated. Jesus said, "I am . . . the life" (John 14: 6); and John affirmed, "He that hath the Son hath life" (1 John 5: 12). By the Spirit, Christ comes to dwell within the heart, and *eternal life* is begun! "It is the Holy Ghost who is here called 'the Spirit of life,' as opening up in the souls of believers fountains of spiritual life" (JFB Commentary). "*Fountains* of spiritual life" is an apt metaphor, for our Lord Himself stated, "He that believeth on Me, as the Scripture hath said, out of his belly (his inner man) shall flow rivers of living water"—on which John comments, "This spake He of the Spirit, which they that believe on Him should receive: for the Holy Ghost was not yet given: because that Jesus was not yet glorified" (John 7: 38, 39). This expresses the perennial welling-up of grace within the heart by the Spirit, like a living fountain of water, adequate and ever-fresh, to meet every need of daily life, in all the pilgrimage from conversion onwards. The same thought is conveyed by the most precious of the names of the Spirit, given by our Lord to the disconsolate disciples as He told them of His impending departure—

(xvi) THE COMFORTER (John 14: 16; 15: 26). The full value of this name lies in the insistence of our Lord that, by the Spirit, *He* would be with them still: He would not leave them desolate, as orphans, but would come unto them (John 14: 18). All that He had been to them, He would be still, by the Spirit. Well is He named "the Comforter"; but that word does not express all that *Paracletos* means. This word is used by John concerning Christ Himself, and is translated in the A.V., "Advocate" (1 John 2: 1). Literally it means, "one called alongside to help." Inexhaustible wealth of promise and assurance is contained within that word (see p. 155). It means that He is *ever present* with the believer; and ever present *to help*, to be all that Christ in His wondrous grace is. The Spirit brings the presence, the resources, of the Lord Himself.

· Here is more than enough to meet every demand of life upon the Christian! Something of the length and breadth and depth and height of the riches of grace in Christ and by the Spirit are hinted at in such further titles as were given prophetically in Isaiah 11: 2—"the Spirit of understanding, of counsel and might, the Spirit of knowledge and of the fear of the Lord." This is the "Spirit of the Lord" which Isaiah foretold should rest upon the Messiah; and this same Spirit in His manifold gifts and grace is now bestowed upon us. We have not been given a spirit of fear, says Paul, but of power, and of love, and of a sound mind (2 Tim. 1: 7). By the Spirit the full potentialities of our manhood, created in the image and likeness of

God, may be realized; nay more, we may become conformed to the image of Christ Himself (Rom. 8: 29; 12: 2), for "we all, with open face beholding as in a mirror the glory of the Lord, are changed into the same image from glory to glory, even as by the Spirit of the Lord" (2 Cor. 3: 18).

Bibliography

BICKNELL, E. J. *The Thirty-Nine Articles*. London: Longmans, Green & Co. 3rd Edition, revised by H. J. Carpenter, 1955.

BIDDULPH, H. *The Names of God*. Booklet. London: Christian Alliance of Women and Girls, n.d.

BRUCE, A. B. *The Training of the Twelve*. Edinburgh: T. & T. Clark. 5th Edn., 1898.

BRUCE, F. F. *Names of God*. Articles in "The Senior Teacher's Magazine." London: Children's Special Service Mission, 1955.
The Sure Mercies of David: A Study in the Fulfilment of Messianic Prophecy. London: Evangelical Library Lecture, 1954.

CUMMING, J. ELDER. *Through the Eternal Spirit*. Stirling: Drummond's Tract Depot, n.d.

DENNEY, JAMES. *Studies in Theology*. London: Hodder & Stoughton. 7th Edn., 1902.

DODS, MARCUS. *Israel's Iron Age*. London: Hodder & Stoughton, 1874.

DYER, WILLIAM. *The Famous Titles of Christ*. Glasgow: Porteous and Hislop, 1863

EDERSHEIM, ALFRED. *The World Before the Flood*; *The Exodus and the Wanderings in the Wilderness*; *Israel under Joshua and the Judges*; *Israel under Samuel, Saul, and David*; *History of Judah and Israel*; London: Religious Tract Society, n.d.

ELLISON, H. L. *The Centrality of the Messianic Idea for the Old Testament*. Booklet. London: Tyndale Press, 1953.
The "Names" of God. Articles in "The Bible Student," India, 1954.

FARRAR, F. W. *The Life of Christ*. London: Cassell & Co., 1886.

FORSYTH, P. T. *The Person and Place of Jesus Christ*. London: Independent Press. 5th Edn., 1948.

GIBSON, J. MONRO. *The Mosaic Era*. London: Hodder & Stoughton 1881.

GIRDLESTONE, R. B. *Synonyms of the Old Testament.* Grand Rapids, Michigan, U.S.A., Wm. B. Erdmans, 1948. A reproduction of the second edition of 1897.

HABERSHON, ADA R. *The New Testament Names and Titles of the Lord of Glory.* London: James Nisbet & Co., 1910.

HAMMOND, T. C. *In Understanding be Men.* London: Inter-Varsity Fellowship. 2nd Edn., 1936.

JENNINGS, F. C. *Studies in Isaiah.* New York: Loizeau Bros., n.d.

JUKES, ANDREW. *The Names of God in Holy Scripture.* London: Longmans, Green & Co., 1888.
The Mystery of the Kingdom. London: Longmans. 3rd Edn., 1884.
Types of Genesis. London: Longmans. 5th Edn., 1885.

KELLY, W. *An Exposition of Isaiah.* London: C. A. Hammond, 1947.

LIDDON, H. P. *The Divinity of Our Lord.* London: Longmans. 22nd Impression, 1908.

MACBEATH, JOHN. *What is His Name?* London: Marshall, Morgan & Scott, Ltd., n.d.

M'INTYRE, D. M. *Christ the Lord.* London: Marshall, Morgan & Scott, Ltd., n.d.

MEYER, F. B. *Christ in Isaiah.* London: Marshall, Morgan & Scott, Ltd. New Edn., 1950.

MORGAN, G. CAMPBELL. *God's Last Word to Man.* London: Marshall, Morgan & Scott, Ltd., n.d.
Great Chapters of the Bible. London: Marshall, Morgan & Scott, Ltd. 2nd Edn., 1946.
Letters of Our Lord. London: Pickering & Inglis, n.d.
Searchlights from the Word. London: Oliphants Ltd. Revised Edn., 1953.
The Spirit of God. London: Westminster Publishing Co., n.d.
This was His Faith: Expository Letters of G. Campbell Morgan, compiled and edited by Jill Morgan. London: Pickering & Inglis., n.d.

MOULE, H. C. G. *Outlines of Christian Doctrine.* London: Hodder & Stoughton. 2nd Edn., 1889.

MURRAY, ANDREW. *The Spirit of Christ.* London: Nisbet & Co. 26th Thousand, n.d.

NEWTON, RICHARD. *Covenant Names and Privileges.* London: R. D. Dickinson, 1883.

NICOLL, W. ROBERTSON. *The Incarnate Saviour.* Edinburgh: T. & T. Clark, 1897.

OWEN, JOHN. *The Glory of Christ.* London: Sovereign Grace Union, 1933.

PARKER, JOSEPH. *The Priesthood of Christ.* London: R. D. Dickinson, 1877.

PLUMTRE, E. H. *The Epistles to the Seven Churches.* London: Hodder & Stoughton, 1884.

PURVES, P. C. *The Jehovah Titles of the Old Testament.* Stirling: Drummond's Tract Depot, n.d.

SANDERS, J. OSWALD. *Christ Incomparable.* London: Marshall, Morgan & Scott, Ltd., 1952.

SCROGGIE, W. GRAHAM. *Psalms.* London: Pickering & Inglis. Revised Edition, 1948.

SEARLE, AMBROSE. *Horae Solitairiae.* Title page missing.

SEISS, J. A. *The Apocalypse.* London: Marshall, Morgan & Scott, Ltd. 15th Edn., n.d.

SMITH, DAVID. *In the Days of His Flesh.* London: Hodder & Stoughton, 1905.

STANDFORD, CHARLES. *The Lord's Prayer.* London: Hodder & Stoughton, 1884.

STANLEY, A. P. *History of the Jewish Church.* London: John Murray, 1906.

TATFORD, F. A. *Prophecy's Last Word.* London: Pickering & Inglis, 1947.

TAYLOR, VINCENT. *The Names of Jesus.* London: Macmillan & Co., 1953.

THIRTLE, J. W. *In the Name.* London: Alfred Holness, n.d.
The Lord's Prayer. London: Morgan & Scott, Ltd., 1915.

THOMAS, W. H. GRIFFITH. *The Principles of Theology.* London: Longmans, Green & Co., 1930.

TRENCH, R. C. *Synonyms of the New Testament.* Cambridge: Macmillan & Co. 2nd Edn., 1854.
The Epistles to the Seven Churches. London: Macmillan & Co. 3rd Edn., 1867.

VINE, W. E. *Expository Dictionary of New Testament Words.* London: Oliphants, 1939.

WARFIELD, B. B. *The Lord of Glory.* London: Hodder & Stoughton, 1907.
The Person and Work of Christ. Philadelphia: Presbyterian & Reformed Publishing Co., 1950.

WEBB-PEPLOE, H. W. *The Titles of Jehovah.* London: Nisbet & Co., 1901.

WESTCOTT, B. F. *The Historic Faith.* London: Macmillan, 1883.
The Revelation of the Father. London: Macmillan, 1884.

YOUNG, EDWARD. J. *Studies in Isaiah.* London: Tyndale Press, 1954.

Commentaries Consulted:
Matthew Henry
A Commentary for English Readers, Edited by C. J. Ellicott.
A Commentary on the Whole Bible, by Jamieson, Fausset, and Brown.
The New Bible Commentary, Edited by F. Davidson, A. M. Stibbs, and E. F. Kevan.
Cambridge Bible for Schools.
Horne's Commentary on the Psalms.
The Treasury of David, by C. H. Spurgeon.
George Adam Smith—Isaiah, Jeremiah, The Twelve Prophets.
G. Campbell Morgan—Jeremiah, Matthew, Mark, Luke, John.
H. C. G. Moule—Romans, Ephesians, Philippians, Colossians.
B. F. Westcott—John's Gospel, Ephesians, Hebrews, John's Epistles.
J. B. Lightfoot—Galatians, Philippians, Colossians.
Martin Luther—Galatians.
T. C. Edwards—1 Corinthians.
Alexander MacLaren—Colossians, Philemon.
Norval Gueldenhuys—Luke.
David Baron—Zechariah.
J. B. Mayor—James.

Critical and Expository Cyclopaedia, A. R. Fausset.
International Standard Bible Encyclopaedia, Edited by James Orr.

Index

Abba (Father), 94, 180
Abhir (Mighty One), 30
Adon (Lord), 25
Adonai (Lord), 25
Adonai Jehovah (Lord GOD), 20
Adoption, Spirit of, 180
Advocate (*see also* Paraclete), 155
Almighty, 37
Alpha and Omega, 163
Amen, 166
Angel of the LORD, 101
Anointed, 114
Apostle and High Priest, 157
Author and Finisher of Faith, 142
Author of Salvation, 142

Banner, The LORD is my, 67
Beginning of the Creation of God, 166
Beloved, 144
Bishop of our Souls, 152
Branch, 103
Bread, Living, 160
Bridegroom, 151
Bright and Morning Star, 168
Buckler, 30

Captain of Salvation, 142
Chereb (Sword), 30
Chiefest Among Ten Thousand, 101
Chosen of God, 145
Choter (Rod), 104
Christ, 114, 143
Comforter, 155, 181
Coming One, 132
Counsellor, 106

David, He that hath the Key of, 165

David, Root of, 166
David, Son of, 133
Desire of all Nations, 108
Despotēs (Master), 129
Didaskalos (Teacher), 128
Door of the Sheep, 153

Ebenezer, 60
Effulgence of the Divine Glory, 147
Elect of God, 108, 145
El (God), 18
El-Bethel (God of Bethel), 35
El-Elohe-Israel (God the God of Israel), 34
El Elyon (Most High God), 42
El Gibbor (Mighty God), 30, 106
Eloah (God), 19
Elohim (God), 16
El Olam (Everlasting God), 45
El Roi ("Thou God Seest Me"), 48
El Shaddai (God Almighty), 37
Elyon (Most High), 42
Ensign, 68
Epistatēs (Master), 129
Eternal Spirit, 177
Everlasting Father, 107
Everlasting God, 45

Faith, Spirit of, 179
Faithful and True, 166
Faithful Witness, 162
Father, 94
Father, Spirit of your, 180
First and Last, 163
Firstbegotten of the Dead, 162
Firstborn, 149
Fortress, 29

Messiah, 114, 132
Metsudah (Fortress), 29
Mighty One, Mighty God, 30, 106
Morning Star, 168
Most High God, 42
M'qaddishkhem (Sanctifieth), 71

Name of Jesus, 15
Name of the LORD, 14
Nes (Ensign), 68
Netsach (Strength), 32
Netzer (Branch), 104
Nissi (Banner), 67

Oikodespotēs (Householder), 129
Olam (Everlasting), 45
Only Begotten, 149

Paraclete, 155, 181
Peace, Prince of, 107
Peace, The LORD send, 75
Priest, High, 156
Prince of Life, 142
Prince of Peace, 107
Prince of the Kings of the Earth, 162
Promised One, 133
Prophet, 103, 114, 134
Propitiation, 139
Provide, the LORD will, 55

Rabbi, 127
Rabboni, 128
Rapha (Healeth), 61
Redeemer, 137
Resurrection and the Life, 141
Righteous One, 146
Righteousness, The LORD our, 85, 146
Rock, 28
Rod, 104
Rohi (Shepherd), 81
Roi (Vision), 48
Root of David, 166
Rose of Sharon, 101
Ruler of the Kings of the Earth, 162

Sabaoth (Hosts), 51
Sanctifieth, The LORD that, 71
Saviour, 137
Second Man, 141
Sela (Rock), 29
Sent One, 133
Servant of the LORD, 108
Seven Spirits of God, 165, 177
Shaddai (Almighty), 37
Shalom (Peace), 75
Shammah (The LORD is There), 89
Shepherd, 81, 152
Shield, 30
Shiloh (He whose right it is), 102
Son of Abraham, 133
Son of David, 133
Son of God, 123
Son of Joseph, 111
Son of Man, 120
Son of Mary, 111
Son of the Blessed, 125
Son of the Highest, 123
Spirit of Adoption, 180
Spirit of Christ, 176
Spirit of Faith, 179
Spirit of Glory, 174
Spirit of God, 171
Spirit of Grace, 179
Spirit of Holiness, 178
Spirit of Jesus, 176
Spirit of Life, 180
Spirit of the Living God, 174
Spirit of Truth, 179
Spirit of Wisdom, 178
Spirit of your Father, 180
Spirit, The Eternal, 177
Spirit, The Holy, 178
Standard, 68
Star, Morning, 168
Stone, 157
Strength of Israel, 32
Sword, 30

Teacher, 128
True, The, 165
True Vine (*see* Vine)
Truth, Spirit of, 179

parlous

Catena
apposite